BASIC GOALS IN
SPELLING

SEVENTH EDITION

WILLIAM KOTTMEYER AND AUDREY CLAUS

Webster Division, McGraw-Hill Book Company

New York   St. Louis   San Francisco   Dallas   Atlanta

William Kottmeyer, former Superintendent of the St. Louis Public Schools, is a nationally recognized educational innovator. His spelling and reading publications have received high acclaim for nearly four decades. Dr. Kottmeyer is currently an author-in-residence in the Webster Division.

Audrey Claus is a former teacher and administrator in the St. Louis Public Schools. Miss Claus is co-author of five editions of this spelling series and several reading programs. She, too, is currently an author-in-residence in the Webster Division.

Project Director: Virginia S. Brown
Sponsoring Editor: Neysa Chouteau
Editing Supervisors: Sue Watson McCormick and Robert Towns
Designers: E. Rohne Rudder and Donna M. Stephens
Production Manager: Tom Goodwin

The photos in this book are by Carol Barry, 135; Gary Brady, 116, 121, 122; Walter Chandoha, 21, 81, 84, 85, 117, 172, 173, 175, 185; Paul Chesley, 31; *Bruce Coleman/* Jane Burton, 156, 160; M.P.L. Fogden, 100; R.E. Pelham, 126, 129; E.R. Degginger, 26, 41, 42; Al Gardner, 106, 109, 110; *Grant Heilman/* Barb Runk, 131, 132, 134; Runk/ Schoenberger, 151; Dwight Kuhn, 45, 61, 111, 112, 115, 146, 147; Robert Lee III, 36, 76, 80, 170; Don Massey, 120; Frank Oberle, Jr., cover, 1, 2, 3, 4, 5, 6, 7, 10, 11, 12, 15, 20, 22, 25, 32, 35, 37, 40, 46, 47, 50, 51, 55, 56, 57, 60, 62, 65, 70, 72, 75, 86, 87, 90, 91, 92, 94, 95, 96, 97, 100, 101, 102, 105, 125, 136, 138, 142, 145, 150, 152, 155, 158, 161, 163, 165, 166, 176, 177, 180, 186, 188; *Photo Researchers/*Ken Highfill, 66; M.E. Warren, 181; St. Louis Zoological Park, 16, 18; Mark Sanderbeck, 67, 171; Robert Silverman, 71; David Tylka, 127, 130.

The illustrations were created by Bill and Judie Anderson and Gordon Willman.
The cover design is by E. Rohne Rudder.

ISBN 0-07-034633-X

TABLE OF CONTENTS

HOW TO WRITE THE ALPHABET

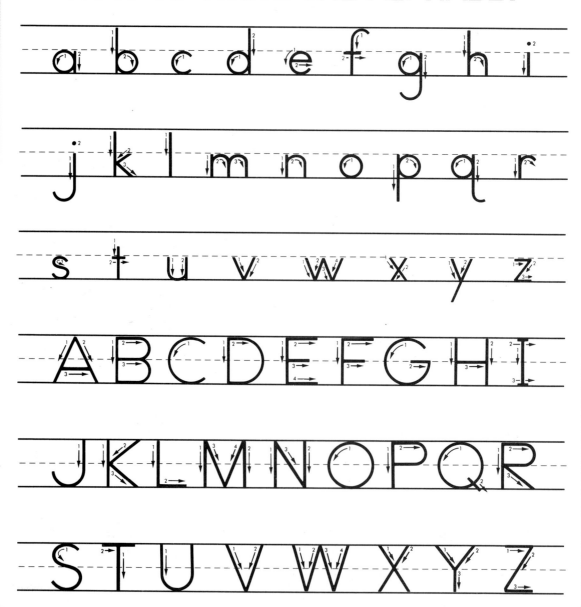

a b c d e f g h i

j k l m n o p q r

s t u v w x y z

A B C D E F G H I

J K L M N O P Q R

S T U V W X Y Z

3

SOUNDS AND LETTERS

Each of these consonant letters spells the starting sound of the key-picture word in the box.

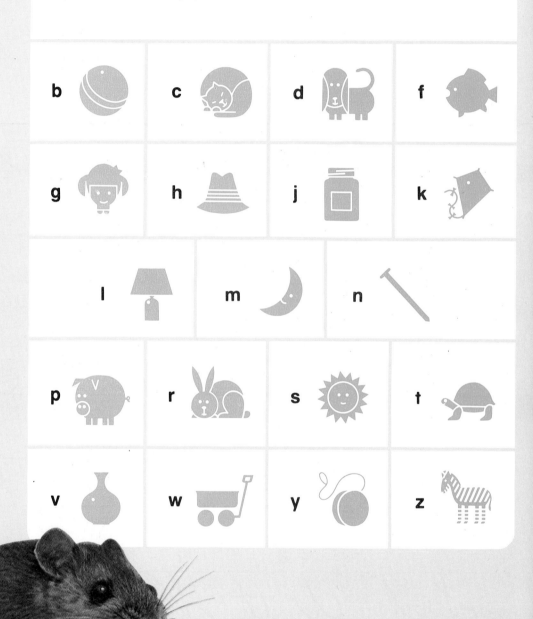

Write the consonant letters that start the key-picture words.

1. _____

2. _____

3. _____

4. _____

5. _____

6. _____

7. _____

8. _____

9. _____

10. _____

11. _____

12. _____

13. _____

14. _____

15. _____

16. _____

17. _____

18. _____

19. _____

glad
stamp
plant
wet
best
kept
trip
fix
list
hunt
dug
just
drop
spot
cost
▽front

The spelling words have short-vowel sounds.

The short-*a* sound is the 🍎 sound in **cat**.

The short-*e* sound is the 🐘 sound in **hen**.

The short-*i* sound is the ⛄ sound in **pig**.

The short-*u* sound is the ☂ sound in **bug**.

The short-*o* sound is the 🐙 sound in **hot**

or the 🦩 sound in **dog.**

1. Say the short-vowel words. Hear the sounds.

2. Write the words with the short-**a** sound.

3. Write the short-**e** words and the short-**i** words.

4. Write the short-**o** words and the short-**u** words.

A snurk is a word that is not spelled the way it sounds.
Say front. What short-vowel sound do you hear? Why do we call front a snurk?

5. Write **front, just,** and **cost.**

Draw a line under the word with

the sound.

Working with the Words

1. Write **trips** and .

glad
stamp
plant
wet
best
kept
trip
fix
list
hunt
dug
just
drop
spot
cost

front

2. Write **hunt, cost, kept,** and **fix.**
Draw lines under the words with
the same starting sound.

3. Write **dug, drop, glad,** and **best.** Draw a line
under the word with the  sound.

4. Write the spelling word for each meaning.

   a. let slip   **b.** mend   **c.** not back

5. Write sentences. Use five words in each
sentence. Use the period at the end.

       lift   lot   plant   The

a.

       cost   a   .   costs

      hat   .   get   got

b.

    hunt   best   His   wet

Building Spelling Power

1. Change the short-vowel spellings to make new words. Write the new words.

a. Write **trip** and . **b.** Write **dug** and .

c. Write **fix** and .

2. Change the starting letters to spell new words.

a. Write **lift** and . **b.** Write **cost** and .

c. Write **trip** and .

Dictionary Help

/a/ shows the vowel sound in **cat.**

/e/ shows the vowel sound in **hen.**

/i/ shows the vowel sound in **pig.**

/o/ shows the vowel sound in **hot.**

/ô/ shows the vowel sound in **dog.**

/u/ shows the vowel sound in **bug.**

Spelling Helps Reading

Sound out these short-vowel words.

back	swept	box	belt	bus	cut	camp
slept	drag	drum	dust	flag	fox	gift
hand	log	nest	job	six	tent	crop
lamp	melt	next	rock	frog	test	twins

Choose the **B** word that goes with the **A** words.
Tell why.

	A			**B**	
1. leg	hip	neck	grand	hand	risk
2. hat	belt	sock	pin	slot	cap
3. sled	blocks	top	drum	log	pig
4. pot	tub	pan	jug	plant	flap
5. frog	cat	fox	tent	nest	dog
6. bed	lamp	rug	mop	desk	bus
7. jump	run	hop	sit	skip	rest
8. milk	buns	crust	tin	ham	bug
9. Fred	Ben	Dan	Sam	Peg	Nan
10. stamp	camp	damp	stump	limp	tramp

We hear the sound and write the letter.
It makes us spell short-vowel words better.

Test

10

beg

2 Odd Egg

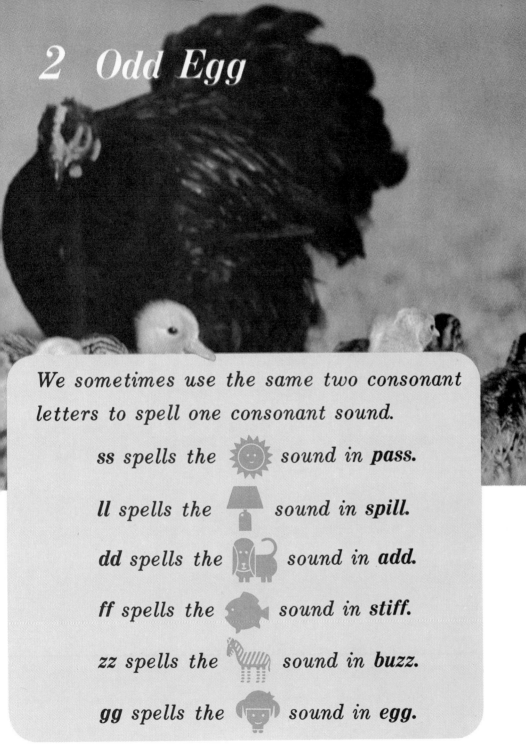

add
pass
class
less
spell
egg
stiff
spill
kiss
doll
toss
odd
cuff
buzz
dull

We sometimes use the same two consonant letters to spell one consonant sound.

ss spells the ☀ sound in **pass.**

ll spells the 🛋 sound in **spill.**

dd spells the 🐕 sound in **add.**

ff spells the 🐟 sound in **stiff.**

zz spells the 🦓 sound in **buzz.**

gg spells the 👧 sound in **egg.**

 1. Write the words that <u>end</u> with the sound.

11

2. Write the words that end with the  sound.

3. Write the words that end with **gg**, **zz**, and **ff**.

4. Write a spelling word for each picture.

 a.　 b.　c.

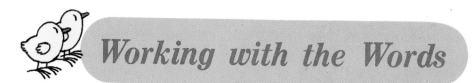

Working with the Words

1. Write the words with the /a/ sound.

2. Write the /o/ words and the /i/ words.
Draw a line under the word that spells 　.

12

3. Write the picture words with **ing** endings.

a.

b.

c.

d.

4. Add **s** to three spelling words to spell "more than one."

a.

b.

c.

We add **es** to words that end in **s** to spell "more than one": **dress — dresses.**

5. Spell "more than one" **class** and **kiss.**

6. Write the words for  and one .

add
pass
class
less
spell
egg
stiff
spill
kiss
doll
toss
odd
cuff
buzz
dull

13

Building Spelling Power

Write the words that go with the pictures.

1.  an odd brass bell

   an add brass bell

2.  some glass on a hill

   some grass on a hill

3.  a cross on a doll dress

   a cross on a dull dress

Dictionary Help

/d/ shows the sound that ends **add.**

/g/ shows the sound that ends **egg.**

/l/ shows the sound that ends **still.**

/f/ shows the sound that ends **stiff.**

/s/ shows the sound that ends **pass.**

/z/ shows the sound that ends **buzz.**

Spelling Helps Reading

Sound out these **Odd Egg** words.

bell	boss	brass	cliff	cross	dress	fell
bill	fill	loss	puff	glass	grass	hill
inn	mill	miss	swell	off	muff	sell
skull	sniff	ill	still	tell	well	smell

"Doing words" are **verbs.** "Naming words" are **nouns.**
Choose three nouns or three verbs in each row.

1.	bell	spill	glass	spin	cliff
2.	add	fell	flag	fill	job
3.	grass	eggs	lift	hill	snip
4.	hop	pill	doll	skull	skip
5.	gift	sell	sniff	spell	tent
6.	mill	jump	class	moss	kiss
7.	muff	nest	dog	melt	dig
8.	lamp	tell	dig	sit	inn

Watch out for words like and !
Double that l and double that s.

Test

15

grab
plan
drag
step
pet
beg
drip
skip
slip
stop
trot
rob
rub
scrub
hug

3 Hug-Hugged-Hugging

When a word ends with one vowel letter and one consonant letter, we double the last consonant letter before we add **ed** or **ing.**

hug   hugged   hugging

 1. Write the /a/ words and the /u/ words.

2. Write the /i/ words and the /o/ words.

3. Write the /e/ words.

4. Write **rob, pet,** and **rub** as **ing** words.

5. Write **skip, hug,** and **scrub** as **ed** words.

Working with the Words

1. Write a verb, or "doing word," for each picture. Then write each word with its **ing** ending.

a.   b.

2. Write these "doing words" from the spelling list with their **ing** endings.

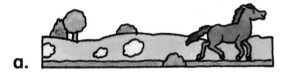

a.

b.

17

grab
plan
drag
step
pet
beg
drip
skip
slip
stop
trot
rob
rub
scrub
hug

3. Write a verb, or "doing word," for each picture. Then write each word with its **ed** ending.

a.    b.

4. Write spelling words with **ed** endings.

a.    b.

5. Write the spelling word for each meaning.

a. ask   **b.** run   **c.** pat

*When a word ends with two consonant letters, we do not double the last letter before we add **ed** or **ing**: **plant, planted, planting.***

6. Write **rest, plan,** and **skip** with **ing** endings.

18

Building Spelling Power

We can use the sounds of key-picture words to spell new words.

+ + = *wag*

/w/ /a/ /g/

1. Write new words. Then write each word with the **ed** and **ing** endings.

   a. + + = ___.

   b. + + + = ___.

2. Write the missing word.

Nell and Bill have been ___.

Sound out these **Hugged-Hugging** words.

begged	getting	planning	stripped	tapped
clapped	grabbed	robbed	sitting	stepped
cutting	hopping	running	stopped	stopping
digging	hugging	scrubbed	slipped	swimming
dropped	hummed	setting	spinning	skipping

Ping!

Boy: How many **p**'s in **hop**? In **hopping**?

Girl: In **shop** and **chop**? In **shopping, chopping**?

Boy: **Mop** and **mopping**? **Drop** and **dropping**?

All: Words like these need more than **ing**.
Words like these must have a **ping**!

Girl: Count the **p**'s in **dip** and **dipping**,

Boy: **Rip** and **ripping**, **tip** and **tipping**,

Girl: **Slip** and **slipping**, **drip** and **dripping**.

All: They simply will not stand for **ing**.
Every one must have a **ping**!

Boy: You may **tap**, but I am **tapping**.

Girl: He may **clap**, but she is **clapping**.

Boy: We may **slap**, but they are **slapping**.

All: It will not do to add just **ing**.
The **p**'s are free, so add the **ping**!

Test

4 Which Fresh Thing

which
when
whip
splash
fresh
shot
path
tenth
thump
strong
swing
thing
branch
inch
chest

 sure

Which Fresh Thing *words have*

two-letter consonant sounds.

*wh spells the sounds that start **which**.*
*ch spells the sound that ends **which**.*
*sh spells the sound that ends **fresh**.*
*th spells the sound that starts **thing**.*
*ng spells the sound that ends **thing**.*

 1. Write the /a/ words and the /i/ words.

which
when
whip
splash
fresh
shot
path
tenth
thump
strong
swing
thing
branch
inch
chest

sure

2. Write the /e/ and /u/ words. Draw lines under the letters that spell two-letter consonant sounds.

3. Write **shot, strong,** and **sure.** Draw lines under the words that start with the  sound.

*Say **sure.** Does s spell /s/?*

Does u spell /u/?

*Why do we call **sure** a snurk?*

Working with the Words

1. Write the picture words.

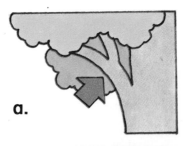

a.

b.

c.

d.

2. Write a snurk to go in this sentence.

They are ___ of winning.

3. Read the sentences. Write each word under the sign for its vowel sound. Skip **the** and **a.**

That chest is six inches long.

This swing hangs on a strong branch.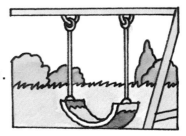

Beth and Bob stepped off the path.

Fred has dropped his fresh eggs.

/a/	/e/	/i/	/o/ or /ô/
That	*chest*		

Building Spelling Power

1. Write **ch** words.

a.  + + + **ch**

b. + + + **ch**

2. Use all the words to write sentences.

a.

| The | to | have |

| wants | . | lunch | king |

b.

| is | at | . | Pat |

| a | ranch |

Spelling Helps Reading

Sound out these **Which Fresh Thing** words.

bath	dish	spring	chill	chin	king
cloth	sixth	bunch	hang	ship	wings
shop	brush	moth	shelf	shell	rush
bench	fish	rang	thrill	chop	fifth

1. One noun in each line does not belong. Find it.

a. whips	branches	inches	chest
b. things	paths	bench	baths
c. chin	dishes	brushes	bunches
d. flashes	kings	moth	lunches
e. ranch	ship	wings	shop

2. One verb in each line does not belong. Find it.

a. splashed	thumped	swing	swung
b. chilled	chopped	fished	hang
c. rang	ring	flashed	whizzed
d. sing	brush	rush	sang
e. sprang	spring	blush	sting

Have a look at what we found.
Write **two** letters! Spell **one** sound!

Test

25

clock
trick
kick
block
wink
drink
drank
skunk
hatch
itch
scratch
switch
quick
quit
quack
 quiet

5 Catch the Quick Skunk

Catch the Quick Skunk words have tricky consonant letters.

tch spells the *sound that ends* **catch.**

qu spells the *sounds that start* **quick.**

ck spells the *sound that ends* **quick.**

n before k spells the *sound in* **skunk.**

 1. Write the six words that end with **ck.**

Circle the words with the sounds.

2. Write the words with the /ng/ sound.
Draw a line under each **nk.**

*Say **quiet.** Hear two word parts, or **syllables.***

*How is **quiet** different from the other **qu** words?*

*Why do we call **quiet** a snurk?*

3. Write **quit, quick,** and **quiet.** Circle the snurk.

4. Write **sure, front,** and **quiet.** Draw a line under
the word that means "still."

 Working with the Words

1. Write the picture words.

a.

b.

c.

clock
trick
kick
block
wink
drink
drank
skunk
hatch
itch
scratch
switch
quick
quit
quack
quiet

2. Write the word for each meaning.

    a. stop   **b.** shut one eye   **c.** fast

3. Write **kick** and **hatch** with **ing** and **ed** endings.

4. Write **switch, itch,** and **drink** with **ing** endings.

5. Write the sentences.

   Use three spelling words.

a.

   He ___ a big glass of milk.

b.

   The duck ___ at a ___.

Building Spelling Power

1. Change the vowel letter of **tricks** to spell new words.

a.    b.

2. Change the starting letters of **drank** to spell new words.

a.    b.

3. Change **scratches** to spell new words.

a.    b.

4. Use two words to tell about each picture: **ducks, clocks, catching, skunks, ticking, quacking.**

a.    b.    c.

Dictionary Help

/k/ stands for the sound that starts and ends **kick.**

Sound out these **Catch the Quick Skunk** words.

think	pink	stretch	tick	match	pack
patch	stick	catch	lock	shrink	witch
squint	black	lick	sank	truck	clock
thank	quilt	quiz	track	crack	sink

Choose the word in each row that does not belong.
Tell why.

1. plank   stick   (truck)   branch   match
2. mink   cat   skunk   rat   dock
3. chick   deck   duck   hen   thrush
4. honk   cluck   quack   lock   clank
5. black   tan   back   pink   red
6. pitch   catch   bat   run   pet
7. tank   crutch   glass   cup   crock
8. quilt   quiz   quick   kick   squint

Do watch the t in **itch** and **witch**.
But skip it, friend, in **which** and **rich**.

Test

30

6 Gray Whale Tail

hay
pay
gray
way
lay
paid
laid
chain
aim
nail
skate
whale
grade
sale
wave
▽ great

The vowel sound in **Gray Whale Tail** words is called the long-**a** sound.

ay spells the long-**a** sound in **gray.**

a with a consonant and **e** spells the long-**a** sound in **whale.**

ai spells the long-**a** sound in **tail.**

1. Say the spelling words. Hear the vowel sounds.

2. Write the **ai** words.

hay
pay
gray
way
lay
paid
laid
chain
aim
nail
skate
whale
grade
sale
wave

great

3. Write the **ay** words.

4. Write the words with **a**-consonant letter-**e.**

5. Write **aim, lay,** and **hay.** Draw a line under the word that starts with a vowel sound.

> Say **great.** Hear the long-**a** sound. Do we spell **great** like the other spelling words? Why do we call **great** a snurk?

6. Write **great** and the words that start like **great.**

7. Write the picture words.

a.   b.   c.

Working with the Words

1. Write three **a**-consonant-**e** picture words.

 **a.**    **b.**   **c.**

2. Use the words to write two sentences.

paid	skate	Ann	and
.	to	Dave	have
to	pay	.	Ray
	his	way	waits

3. Write **lay** and **laid** for these sentences.

    a. Kate ____ the quilt on the bed.

    b. Did Kate ____ it on the bed?

    c. The hen ____ six eggs.

Building Spelling Power

Write the words for each picture.

1.

a snail on a path

a snake on a path

2.

two pails of sand and rocks

two pails of gray paint

3.

four cakes on a tray

four plates of cake

4.

a gate that has been painted

a game that has been played

Dictionary Help   /ā/ shows the long-**a** sound in **gray, whale,** and **tail.**

Spelling Helps Reading

Sound out these **Gray Whale Tail** words.

chase	cake	cane	cape	cave	clay	day
brain	gate	jail	jay	lake	made	maid
pain	plane	paint	plate	pray	rail	spade
snake	shade	rake	sail	tray	vase	sway

Fit the right sentence parts together.
Read the sentences.

1. To make a gray tray red,   I must have a spade.
2. To fix a gate,   I must have paint.
3. To dig up some clay,   I may want a plate.
4. To bake a cake,   I may want nails.

5. To raise a grain crop,   James trains his dog.
6. To wade in a lake,   I must have rain.
7. To make it shake hands,   Ray takes off his socks.
8. To stay safe from flames,   do not play with matches.

You have three ways to spell that /ā/
As in **tail** and **whale** and **gray.**

Test

35

street
teeth
sweet
sweep
cheek
sheet
free
sheep
dream
beat
heat
speak
team
least
each
 dead
 bread

7 Sweet Dream

*The vowel sound in **Sweet Dream** words is called the long-e sound.*

*ee spells the long-e sound in **sweet**.*
*ea spells the long-e sound in **dream**.*

1. Say the spelling words. Hear the vowel sounds.

2. Write the **ea** words with the long-**e** sound.

36

*Say **bread** and **dead**.*

Do you hear the long-e sound?

*Why are **bread** and **dead** snurks?*

3. Write **bread, dead,** and **great.** Draw a line under the words with the /e/ sound.

4. Write the **ee** words.

5. Read the sentence. Write the long-**e** words.

He wants his team to eat some bread.

 Working with the Words

1. Write the words that end with the /k/ sound.

street
teeth
sweet
sweep
cheek
sheet
free
sheep
dream
beat
heat
speak
team
least
each
⬦
dead
bread

2. Write the picture words.

a. _____

b. _____

c. _____

d. _____

3. Write the words with these meanings.

a. brush off

b. say things

c. make hot

d. hit

4. Use the words to write what Jean said.

| the | team | on | must |

| well | Each | do | one |

Jean said,"___."

38

Building Spelling Power

1. Write more **ee** words.

   a. Change **sweep** to .

   b. Change **seen** to .

   c. Change **streets** to .

2. Write more **ea** words.

   a. Change **dream** to .

   b. Change **each** to .

3. Write an **ea** word for each meaning.

   a. not strong   **b.** rich milk   **c.** yell

4. Write an **ee** word for each meaning.

   a. take a nap   **b.** two plus one   **c.** 7 days

Dictionary Help   /ē/ shows the long-e sound in **sweet** and **dream.**

Spelling Helps Reading

Sound out these **Sweet Dream** words.

speech	beach	bee	cream	deep	east	feel
feed	green	keep	lead	lean	leap	meat
need	reach	read	sea	seed	seem	sleep
stream	queen	tea	teach	weak	wheel	mean

In each row, choose two sets of go-together words.

1. three green two gray one pink
2. beets peas peach plum grape beans
3. clean mean cross neat sick fresh
4. leap creep scream jump squeak squeal
5. bee sheep flea skunk moth fox
6. beef cake buns bread ham veal
7. tree grass leaf reeds weeds twig
8. creek stream lake sleet rain hail
9. steel spade brass tin rake brush
10. seed bleed peel sheet leash leap

Most long-**e** words that you will see
We'll spell E-A or just E-E.

Test

8 My Bright Kind Smile

sky
fry
high
bright
grind
wind
prize
shine
slide
fire
pipe
smile
drive
ripe
wife
🔊 child
🔊 wild

*The vowel sound in **My Bright Kind Smile** words is called the long-i sound.*

*y spells the long-i sound in **my**.*
*igh spells the long-i sound in **bright**.*
*i before **nd** spells the long-i sound in **kind**.*
*i with a consonant and e spells the long-i sound in **smile**.*

1. Say the spelling words. Hear the sounds.

41

sky
fry
high
bright
grind
wind
prize
shine
slide
fire
pipe
smile
drive
ripe
wife

child
wild

2. Write the words with **i**-consonant-**e.**

3. Write the words with **y** and with **igh.**

Draw a line under each **y** and **igh.**

4. Write **kind** and the spelling words with **ind.**

> Say **child** and **wild.** Do we spell **child** and **wild** like the other long-i words? Why do we call **child** and **wild** snurks?

5. Write **child, wild,** and **fix.**

Draw a line under the long-**i** words.

6. Write the word for each meaning.

a. grin **b.** gleaming **c.** be bright

42

1. Write the words with these starting sounds.

    a. /ch/   **b.** /sh/

    c. /f/   **d.** /f/

2. Write words that mean "twist" and "slip."

3. Use the words to write what they said.

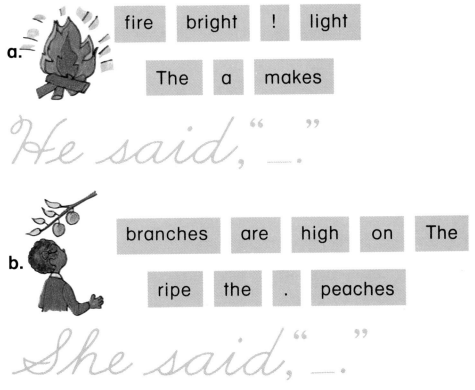

a.

| fire | bright | ! | light |

| The | a | makes |

He said, "___."

b.

| branches | are | high | on | The |

| ripe | the | . | peaches |

She said, "___."

43

Building Spelling Power

1. Write the **i**-consonant-**e** words.

a. one green ____

b.  two straight ____

c. a high ____

d.  pails of ____ paint

2. Write the **igh** words.

a. a bright ____

b. the ____ hand

c. a prize ____

Dictionary Help

/ī/ shows the long-**i** sound in **my** and **bright** and **kind** and **smile.**

44

Spelling Helps Reading

Sound out these long-i words. Then read the story.

sight	blind	cry	dime	dive	fight	strike
quite	five	hide	night	kind	might	fright
rise	mile	mind	spy	time	size	while

A sly fox asked a shy young crane to come to lunch. "Come at nine," he said. "We will have a fine time."

Crane came by the next day. Fox set pie plates on a white cloth. Each plate was filled with cream.

"Eat," cried Fox, as he licked his plate clean.

Crane tried and tried. Just the tip of his bill reached the cream. He did not get a bite to eat.

"Fox," said Crane, "you must dine with ME. Come at five. I will fix a meal you might like."

Fox came on time. Crane had deep vases filled with cream. In went Crane's long, thin bill. He had quite a meal. But Fox had no way to stick his chin in the vase. He did not get one drop of cream.

"My, my," Crane said with a sly smile. "I must not have the right kind of dishes!"

Why do you think Fox made up his mind to quit playing tricks on Crane?

Test

45

sold
scold
throw
snow
grow
float
soak
soap
load
throat
smoke
drove
spoke
broke
rope
▽
none
most

9 Old Show Boat Smoke

DELTA QUEEN

The vowel sound in **Old Show Boat Smoke** words is called the long-**o** sound.

o before **ld** spells the long-**o** sound in **old**.
ow spells the long-**o** sound in **show**.
oa spells the long-**o** sound in **boat**.
o-consonant-**e** spells the long-**o** sound in **smoke**.

1. Say the spelling words. Hear the long-**o** sound. Write the **old** and **oa** words.

2. Write the **ow** words.

3. Write the **o**-consonant-**e** words.
Draw a line under each **o** and circle each **e**.

Say **none** and **most**.

Hear the two different vowel sounds.

Which word <u>looks</u> like a long-**o** word?

Which word <u>sounds</u> like a long-**o** word?

Why do we call **none** and **most** snurks?

4. Write **sure, most, front,** and **none.**
Circle the /u/ words.

Working with the Words

1. Write the words with these meanings.

   a. not sink   **b.** toss   **c.** said

47

sold
scold
throw
snow
grow
float
soak
soap
load
throat
smoke
drove
spoke
broke
rope

ⓢ

none
most

2. Write the spelling words. One is a snurk.

    a. It cleans things.   **b.** It comes from fire.

    c. It is cold and wet.   **d.** It means "not one."

    e. We tie with it.   **f.** It means "fuss."

> We say:
>
> "I **make** it now. I **made** it then.
>
> We **see** it now. We **saw** it last week.
>
> We **ride** now. We **rode** last night."

3. Write a word for each space.

    a. Did she **break** it?

        Yes, she ___ it.

    b. Did he **drive** it?

        Yes, he ___ it.

    c. Did we **ride** fast?

        Yes, we ___ fast.

Building Spelling Power

1. Write the **old** word for each picture.

a.   b. 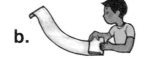    c.

2. Write the words with the same vowel sound.

a. most

cost

cone

b. goat

fold

3. Find one spelling mistake and one other mistake in each sentence. Write the sentences right.

a.    This trick has a full
load of coal

b.    Joan sold five bag bowls

Dictionary Help   /ō/ shows the long-**o** sound in **old** and **show** and **boat**.

49

Sound out these long-**o** words. Then read the story.

those	bowl	blow	coach	coal	coat	woke
hold	gold	goat	goal	fold	cone	cold
hole	hope	joke	hose	nose	old	bold
toast	told	stove	stone	shone	slow	pole

Miss Jones's class had been telling jokes.

"Dad told me an old one," said Rose. "It is not a joke, but a kind of trick. On the road home a man has to cross a stream. He has a dog, a goat, and a sack of oats. His boat can hold him and his dog in one load. It can hold him and his goat. It can hold him and the oats."

Joan Stokes spoke up. "You mean he must row the boat to and fro to get one at a time?"

"Yes, Joan. If the dog is left with the goat, he will have him by the throat in no time. The dog will not eat oats. The goat will. The dog may not be left with the goat. He can be left with the oats. The goat cannot be left with the dog and not with the oats. The trick is to get those three home."

Can you show Rose the way to do it?
How many /ō/ words? Snurks?

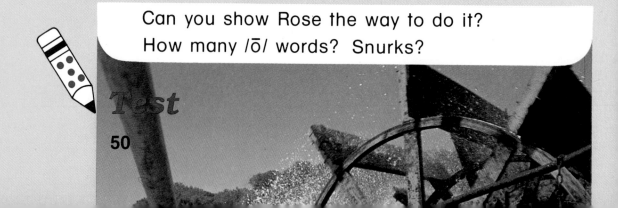

Test

50

10 Bite-Biting

make	making
take	taking
bite	biting
trade	trading
dive	diving
hate	hating
shake	shaking
use	using
wake	waking
wipe	wiping
rule	ruling
⚡ love	loving
⚡ shove	shoving
⚡ lose	losing
⚡ prove	proving

*When a word ends with e, we drop the e before adding **ing**.*

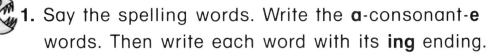

1. Say the spelling words. Write the **a**-consonant-**e** words. Then write each word with its **ing** ending.

making
taking
biting
trading
diving
hating
shaking
using
waking
wiping
ruling

▽

loving
shoving
losing
proving

2. Write the **i**-consonant-**e** words.
Then write each word with its **ing** ending.

> The vowel sound in **use** is called the long-**u** sound. In some words, the long-**u** is the vowel sound we hear in **rule.**

3. Write the **u**-consonant-**e** words.
Then write each word with its **ing** ending.

> Which vowel sound do you hear in **love** and **shove**? In **lose** and **prove**? Which vowel sound does **o**-consonant-**e** spell in most words?

4. Write the **ing** snurk for each picture.

a.

b.

c.

1. Write the opposites. The words are in the list.

    a. finding   **b.** loving   **c.** giving

2. Write **love, shove,** and **prove.** Underline the

snurks with the 🌂 sound.

3. Find one misspelled word and one other mistake
in each sentence. Write the sentences right.

  a.   she is taking a big bit.

  b.   Don and mike are shakeing
                this tree.

Building Spelling Power

1. When a word ends with one vowel letter and one consonant, we double the last consonant before adding **ing**.

hit — hitting   run — running

Write the **ing** words for these pictures.

a.   b.   c.

2. When a word ends with **e,** drop the **e** before **ing.**

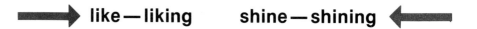
like — liking   shine — shining

Write the **ing** words for these pictures.

a.   b.   c.

Dictionary Help   /ū/ shows the long-**u** sound in **use.**

54

 *Spelling Helps Reading*

Sound out these **ing** words. Then read the verse.

baking	hoping	skating	waving	chasing	raking
smiling	poking	shaping	liking	blaming	hiding
blazing	riding	wading	sliding	racing	choking
piling	shining	grazing	griping	roping	voting

Girl 1: Drop the **e** and add the **ing**
And you'll make the **ing** verbs sing.

Boy 1: Fish are biting, bakers baking,
Divers diving, shakers shaking,

Girl 2: Skaters skating, waders wading,
Voters voting, traders trading,

Boy 2: Smilers smiling, wipers wiping,
Users using, gripers griping,

Girl 3: Hopers hoping, rakers raking,
Flags are waving, makers making,

Boy 3: Cowboys roping, sleepers waking,
Filers filing, takers taking,

Girl 4: Pipers piping, racers racing,
Snipers sniping, chasers chasing!

All: Same old rule. It always works,
Even with those snurky snurks!

 *Test*

jug
joke
jail
age
cage
rage
page
huge
strange
change
large
charge
edge
bridge
judge

11 Huge Bridge Words

g and *j* spell the sound that starts .

ge spells the ending  sound after long-vowel sounds: **huge.**

dge spells the ending  sound after short-vowel sounds: **bridge.**

1. Write the four words that start with the  sound.

2. Write the **dge** words. Draw a line under the short-vowel letters.

3. Write the **ge** words. Circle the words
in which **ge** follows a long-vowel sound.

*Say **large** and **charge**. Hear the vowel
and /r/ sounds. The sounds that
start*  *are spelled **ar**.*

4. Write the words in which **ge** follows a consonant.
Circle the words with the sounds that start .

5. Write two words that mean "big."

6. Write **change** and **charge** with **ing** endings.

a. She is ___ the tire.   **b.** He is ___ a dime.

jug
joke
jail
age
cage
rage
page
huge
strange
change
large
charge
edge
bridge
judge

Working with the Words

These words are in **alphabetical order:**

jail **joke** **jug**

When words start with the same letter, we use the second letter to tell which word comes first.

1. Write the seven /ā/ words in alphabetical order.

2. Write one word for each meaning.

a. odd **b.** switch

c. rim **d.** large

3. Write the picture words.

a.

b.

c.

1. Change the starting letters to spell new words.

a. Change **page** to .

b. Change **keep** to .

c. Change **let** to .

d. Change **jail** to .

2. Write the question. Use the question mark.

| have | fudge | ? | I |

| May | pieces | of | two |

Madge asked, "___"

Dictionary Help

/j/ shows the sound in **judge**.

Sound out these words. Then read the story.

badge	fudge	jam	job	ledge	stage
barge	dodge	jeans	just	jog	trudge
budge	hedge	jet	junk	jeep	lodge

Jack and Madge Page's dad had just changed jobs. The new job was on a barge and it paid high wages. He was in charge of a huge crane that dredged up mud and sludge from the bed of a deep stream.

One day he left his lunch box at home.

"Jack," said Mrs. Page, "take Dad's lunch to him. Madge, put on those jeans and go with Jack."

Jack and Madge trudged off with the lunch box. The two ran to the edge of the stream.

"I see Dad!" cried Madge. "His barge is right at that low bridge that crosses the stream."

"That barge is a long way off," said Jack. "We have no boat. Dad has no boat. His boss will not want to bring the barge in. I cannot throw the box from the bank. We just cannot get the lunch box to him."

"Come on, Jack," cried Madge. "I will show you the way."

Can <u>you</u> tell the way?

Test

60

12 Nice Mice

ice
nice
twice
mice
rice
slice
race
face
place
space
dance
chance
fence
since
voice
once

We use both **s** and **c** to spell the ☀ sound.

saw   1¢ cent

We use **s, ss,** and **ce** to spell the ☀ sound at the end of words.

bus   glass   mice

1. Say the Nice Mice words. Hear the ending sound.

2. Write the /ī/ words. Circle the **ce.**

3. Write the four /ā/ words. Circle the **ce.**

61

ice
nice
twice
mice
rice
slice
race
face
place
space
dance
chance
fence
since
voice
▽ⓢ
once

Say **voice**. Hear the vowel sound. We use **oi** to spell the vowel sound in **voice**. We use **oy** to spell the vowel sound in **boy**.

4. Write **voice, dance, chance, fence,** and **since.**

Draw a line under the /a/ words.

Say **once.** Hear the /u/ sound. Do you hear a starting consonant sound? Why is **once** a snurk?

5. Write **once, fence, sure,** and **front.**

Draw a line under each snurk.

6. Write the words in which **s** spells the ☼ sound.

1. Write the words that start with these sounds.

    a. /s/   **b.** /s/

    c. /s/   **d.** /ch/

    e. /ī/   **f.** /d/

    g. /f/   **h.** /f/

2. Find one mistake in each sentence.
Write the sentences right.

a.  It would be nice to win the rice.

b.  The mice got in a fine save place.

Building Spelling Power

1. The words **dance, race,** and **slice** can be used as verbs. Write **dance, race,** and **slice** with **ing** endings. Be sure to drop the **e** in each word.

2. Add **s** to **face** to spell .

3. Write **rice**. Change **r** to **pr** and to **sp** and write two new words. Circle the word for "cost."

4. Write **since**. Change **s** to **m** and to **pr** and write two new words. Circle the word for "chop up."

5. Write **voice**. Change **v** to **ch** and write a new word.

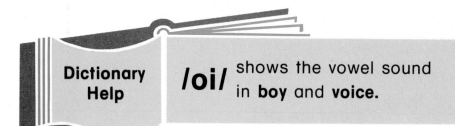

Dictionary Help /oi/ shows the vowel sound in **boy** and **voice**.

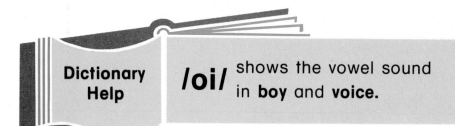

64

Spelling Helps Reading

"The ice is twice as slick since we left," said Bruce, glancing at the road. "Have we a chance to get home?"

"Face it, Bruce," said his dad, Mr. Vance. "This old truck could not win a race, but...." BANG!

Mr. Vance groaned. "A flat!" he cried. "And right on the old bridge! Lace up that nice fleece-lined coat, Bruce, and give me a hand at once."

He jacked up the truck and twisted off the five lugs that held the wheel. He placed them in the hubcap on the fence rail. Bruce danced and stamped to stay warm.

"O.K.," cried Mr. Vance, his voice shaking from the cold. "Hand me the lugs, Bruce."

But just then the wind sent the hubcap flying. The five lugs sank in the stream.

"We needed at least three lugs to hold the wheel on tight," cried Mr. Vance.

"Dad," said Bruce, "why not...."

Test

else
tease
raise
leave
sense
noise
geese
sneeze
twelve
solve
sleeve
please

paste
taste
waste

13 Twelve Geese Words

Twelve Geese words have an extra silent e at the end.

1. Say the words in the spelling list. Hear the sounds.

2. Write the four short-vowel words. Draw a line under each silent **e.**

3. Write the words in which two vowel letters together spell a long-vowel sound.

66

Say waste, taste, and paste. Hear the vowel sound. Which letter spells the /ā/ sound in each word? Why do we call the words snurks?

4. Write the four /ā/ words.
Draw a line under each of the snurks.

5. Write **noise, raise,** and **please.**
Draw a line under the /oi/ word.

 ## *Working with the Words*

1. Write the picture words. Draw a line under the noun that names "more than one."

a.

b.

c.

2. Write the word for each meaning.

a. glue **b.** ten plus two **c.** go

else
tease
raise
leave
sense
noise
geese
sneeze
twelve
solve
sleeve
please

▽

paste
taste
waste

3. Write the word for each meaning.

a. make bad use of

b. eat just a bit

c. play tricks on

d. lift

4. Write the spelling words that fit the sentences.

a.
Do not make
so much ___, ___.

b.
I can ___ it.
Who ___ can do it?

c.
This dog has
a fine ___ of smell.

d.
They ___ fine ___.

Building Spelling Power

We do not always add **s** or **es** to nouns to spell "more than one." Sometimes we write new words.

 man   men

1. Write the "more than one" picture words.

   a.      b.      c.

2. Write **leaves, elves,** and **loaves.** Circle the /ē/ word.

3. Write two words from Exercise 2 to fill the spaces.

These ___ have three huge ___ of bread.

Dictionary Help

/t/ shows the sound that starts **tease** and **twelve.**

/p/ shows the sound that starts **paste** and **please.**

69

Spelling Helps Reading

Sound out these words.

bathe	maize	pulse	shelves	grease	breathe
crease	breeze	praise	cheese	dense	heave
elves	clothes	rinse	weave	bruise	selves
lease	squeeze	loaves	ease	leaves	freeze

Write **T** for **true** or **F** for **false** for each sentence.

1. Five coats are sure to have at least twelve sleeves.
2. Wild geese like to fly east when it gets cold.
3. Mice love the taste of a piece of cheese.
4. Those who want to make peace should be praised.
5. You can freeze grape juice with one ice cube.
6. If you sneeze once, you must have a cold.
7. Soft voices make lots of noise.
8. It is a waste of time to paste stamps on mail.

Bath to **bathe** and **breath** to **breathe**,
And **cloth** to **clothes**, dear, if you **pleathe**.

Test

14 Cool Wool

boot
cool
tooth
pool
noon
broom
roof
shoot
hook
brook
poor
shook
stood
wool
cook
truth

oo spells the vowel sound in *and* **cool.**

oo spells the vowel sound in 📘 *and* **wool.**

1. Write the words with the vowel sound in 📘 .

2. Write the words with the vowel sound in 🌙 .

*Say **truth**. Hear the vowel sound.*

*Does **truth** sound like a Cool word?*

*Does **truth** have an **oo** spelling?*

*Why do we call **truth** a snurk?*

3. Write **truth, took,** and **tooth.**
Circle the words with the same vowel sound.

4. Write **shook, shoot,** and **hook.**
Circle the words with the same vowel sound.

 *Working with the Words*

1. Write the picture words in alphabetical order.

2. Write the picture words in alphabetical order.

3. Write the word for each meaning.

a. fleece from sheep   **b.** not rich

c. not hot, not cold   **d.** a stream

e. top of house   **f.** kind of shoe

We say:

"I **give** it now. I **gave** it then.

He **breaks** it now. He **broke** it then.

You **are** good. You **were** good."

4. Use spelling words to fill the spaces.

a.
Did they **stand** up?

Yes, they ___ up.

b.
Did she **shake** it?

Yes, she ___ it.

c.
He did not tell a lie.

He told the ___ .

d.
Did I ___ straight?

You **shot** straight.

boot
cool
tooth
pool
noon
broom
roof
shoot
hook
brook
poor
shook
stood
wool
cook
truth

73

Building Spelling Power

1. Write the picture words.

a.   b.   c.

2. Find the mistakes. Write the sentences the right way.

a.   The book is too Big.

b.   The crook is chasing the poor goose?

Dictionary Help

/ü/ shows the vowel sound in  and **cool.**

/u̇/ shows the vowel sound in and **wool.**

74

Spelling Helps Reading

Sound out these **Cool Wool** words.

Then read the verse.

bloom	book	goose	booth	choose	food	foot
good	hood	loop	hoof	moon	proof	room
smooth	scoop	took	spool	wood	zoo	stool
troop	tool	too	crook	loose	spoon	fool

LOOK!

I see nice words like **pool** and **tool**
And **fool** and **stool** and **school** and **spool.**

I find I have no spelling r~~ool~~ rule
When I see **boot** and **shoot** and **tooth,**
And meet a pretty girl named R~~ooth~~ Ruth.

I see **noon** and **spoon** and **moon,**
But pretty soon I find it's J~~oon~~ June.

I see **loop** and **stoop** and **droop,**
But have to **scoop** flies from my s~~oop~~ soup.

So when you **look** at **book** and **cook,**
Be sure you take a **good** hard **look.**
When you see words like **stood** and **wood,**
Be sure to spell them as you sh~~ood~~ should.

Test

tall
small
hall
wall
salt
false
fault
cause
law
jaw
yawn
paw
shawl
crawl
lawn

15 Small Maud's Shawl

au *spells the vowel sound in* **Maud.**

aw *spells the vowel sound in* **shawl.**

a *before* **l** *spells the vowel sound in* **small.**

 1. Say the spelling words. Hear the  sound.

2. Write the two **au** words. Draw a line under the word with silent **e.**

3. Write the words with **a** before l. Draw lines under the words with double consonants.

76

4. Write the **aw** words. Draw lines under
the words that end with a vowel sound.

5. Write the picture words.

a.

b.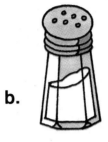

c.

d.

Working with the Words

1. Write the picture verb with **s, ed,** and **ing** endings.

2. Write the word for each meaning.

   a. high   **b.** not true   **c.** side of a room

tall
small
hall
wall
salt
false
fault
cause
law
jaw
yawn
paw
shawl
crawl
lawn

We use an apostrophe to show owning.

Maud's shawl   the cat's paw

Maud owns the shawl.

The cat owns the paw.

3. Write the sentences.

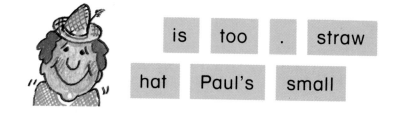

is   too   .   straw

hat   Paul's   small

lawn   ?   Why   the

cutting   is   she

4. Write the word for each meaning.

    a. creep   **b.** a rule

    c. not true   **d.** not large

    e. chin bone   **f.** cat's foot

Building Spelling Power

1. Change the starting letters to write new words.

a. Change **law** to .

b. Change **law** to .

c. Change **yawn** to .

d. Change **salt** to .

e. Change **tall** to .

2. Write the sentence with the missing **aw** and **al** words. Use commas between the words.

He sells ___, ___, a ___, and a ___.

Dictionary Help /ô/ shows the vowel sound in **Maud, small,** and **shawl.**

79

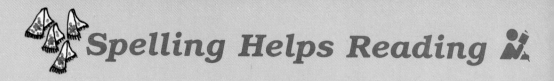
Sound out these /ô/ words. Then read the story.

bald	call	caw	claw	fawn	dawn	drawn
haul	haunt	malt	sauce	saw	stall	hawk
halt	pause	raw	straw	fall	thaw	squawk

"Caw! Caw! Caw!"

"What is that, Aunt Maud?" called Paul.

"That is Jim, the crow," said Paul's aunt. "I leave a loaf of stale bread on the front lawn. At dawn, just when the sun rises, Jim claws it to pieces. He must be squawking at Flag. He thinks he should have all of it."

"Flag? Who—or what—is Flag?" asked Paul.

Just then he caught sight of a small tan thing with long thin legs trotting from the woods.

"That is Flag," said Aunt Maud. "She is quite tame. I taught Flag to lick salt from my hand. She has big, sad eyes and tan skin with white spots. She will pause to eat and then to sleep in that straw pile. So, Paul, when you go home, tell Mom and Dad that you saw a........"

How many /ô/ words? Snurks?

Test

80

16 Loud Crowd

crowd
town
drown
growl
frown
clown
mouse
loud
ground
round
proud
shout
cloud
mouth
count

Loud Crowd words have the vowel sound

that starts 🦉 .

*ou spells the vowel sound in **loud**.*

*ow spells the vowel sound in **crowd**.*

1. Write the **ou** words.
Circle the word with silent **e**.

2. Write the **ow** words.
Circle the words that start with /k/.

3. Write the words that start with these sounds.

    a. /t/   **b.** /sh/

    c. /l/   **d.** /d/

 Working with the Words

1. Change one word in each sentence to make it fit the picture. Write the sentences right.

a.   Why does that clown smile?

b.   This owl is cute.

2. Write the spelling word for each meaning.

a. soil

b. full of pride

c. not soft

d. not smile

To put words in alphabetical order when
the first two letters are the same,
use the third letter:

    ouch   **out**

To put words in alphabetical order when
the first three letters are the same,
use the fourth letter:

    cloud   **clown**

3. Write the picture words in alphabetical order.

4. Write **town, loud,** and **cloud** in alphabetical order.

crowd
town
drown
growl
frown
clown
mouse
loud
ground
round
proud
shout
cloud
mouth
count

83

Building Spelling Power

Remember: ow can spell /ō/, too:

blow   grow

1. Write these **ow** words with the /ō/ sound.

 a.

 b.

 c.

2. Write the **ow** picture words.

 a.

 b.

 c.

3. Write the **ou** picture words.

 a.

 b.

 c.

Dictionary Help

/ou/ shows the vowel sound in **loud** and **crowd**.

84

 ## *Spelling Helps Reading*

Sound out the words. Then read the story.

how	couch	now	mouse	ouch	howl	scout
out	house	owl	bounce	down	pound	sound
cow	pouch	our	brown	plow	hound	trout

"I am thinking of a thing with an /ou/ sound," said Jane. "It lives, so it is not a house, a cloud, a couch."

"Does it hoot? Does it give milk?" asked Jack.

"No, it is not an owl and not a cow."

"Does it like cheese? Do cats pounce on it?" asked Ann. "Does it have a snout? Is it stout?"

"No, it is not a mouse and it is not a sow."

"I have it!" shouted Paul. "It makes a growling sound. It howls at night. It goes out hunting."

"No, it is not a hound, Paul."

"Does it swim?" asked Mike. "Is it good to eat?"

"It is not a trout, Mike."

"Well," said Jane, "it comes to town once in a while. It is funny. It paints its face. Now, what is it?"

/ou/ words? Snurks?

 *Test*

17 Tough Group Snurks

- ▽ ought
- ▽ bought
- ▽ fought
- ▽ brought
- ▽ thought
- ▽ fourth
- ▽ course
- ▽ pour
- ▽ group
- ▽ soup
- ▽ through
- ▽ though
- ▽ touch
- ▽ rough
- ▽ tough

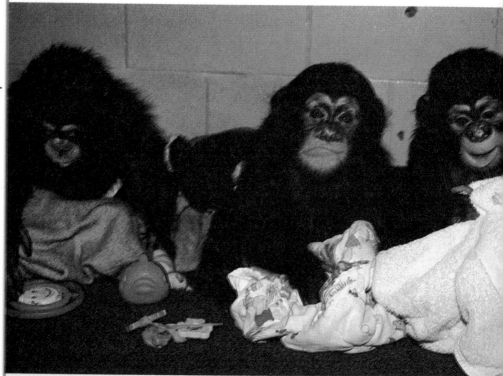

Tough Group *snurks have* **ou** *spellings but no /ou/ sounds.*

Tough Group *snurks have these vowel sounds:*

/u/ *as in* **up**   /ô/ *as in* **off**

/ü/ *as in* **two**   /ō/ *as in* **old**

1. Write the Tough Group words with the /u/ sound.

2. Write the Tough Group words with the /ü/ sound.

3. Write the words with the same /ôr/ sounds as .

4. Write the **ough** words with the /ô/ sound.

5. Write **slow, smoke,** and the Tough Group word with the /ō/ sound.

 Working with the Words

gh spells the /f/ sound in two spelling words.
gh is silent in seven spelling words.
Say the gh words with the /f/ sound.
Say the words with silent gh.

1. Write the words in which **gh** spells the /f/ sound.

2. Write **ought** and the other words with silent **gh.**

ought
bought
fought
brought
thought
fourth
course
pour
group
soup
through
though
touch
rough
tough

3. Write spelling words to fit the sentences.

a.  She will ___ ___ in the bowl.

b.  The young man is rowing ___ ___ waves.

c.  Of ___ you should not ___ a hot stove.

d.  They like the meat ___ it is ___.

4. Write **tough, thought, fourth,** and **though** in alphabetical order.

Building Spelling Power

We say: "I **do** it now. I **did** it then.

I **see** it now. I **saw** it then."

1. Write the missing words.

a.

Did she **buy** it?

Yes, she ___ it.

b.

Did they **fight?**

Yes, they ___.

c.

Did he **bring** your mail?

Yes, he ___ it.

d.

Did you **think** you
would win?
Yes, I ___ I would win.

2. Write the 2 misspelled words right.

a.  tuch   **b.**  soop   **c.** boot

**Dictionary
Help**   **/r/** shows the sound that starts **rough.**

Say these **Tough Group** Snurks. Then read the verse.

thought	rough	four	you	course
bought	tough	fourth	your	young
fought	group	though	pour	touch
brought	soup	dough	tour	through

Teacher: I have been thinking all this week,
We **ought** to spell the way we speak.

Girls: If we can say those sounds like **awt**,
Why must we spell them **bought** and **brought**?
And also **fought**? (That's what I **thought**!)

Boys: If we say **groop**, why spell it **group**?
And then there's **soop**. Why spell it **soup**?
Why do they let us roll a **hoop**?
Or make our wilted flowers **droop**?
And then we have both **through** and **though**,
And **touch** and **pour** and **course** and **dough**.

All: I say they make it mighty **tough**.
It's time to stop. I've had **enough**!
Oh, they do sneak and they do lurk!
I've had it with this O-U snurk.

Test

18 Her First Purse

dirt
shirt
skirt
whirl
perch
verse
jerk
burn
church
nurse
purse
♥ earn
♥ learn
♥ search
♥ earth

All **Her First Purse** words have the same vowel-**r** sounds.

er spells the vowel-**r** sounds in **her**.
ir spells the vowel-**r** sounds in **first**.
ur spells the vowel-**r** sounds in **purse**.

1. Say the **er** words. Write them.

dirt
shirt
skirt
whirl
perch
verse
jerk
burn
church
nurse
purse

S

earn
learn
search
earth

2. Say the **ir** words. Write them.

3. Say the **ur** words. Write them.

> Say **earn, learn, earth,** and **search.** Do they sound like Her First Purse words? Why do we call them snurks?

4. Write the snurks.

Working with the Words

1. Write the words that start with these sounds. Circle the word that means "spin fast."

    a. /ch/   **b.** /hw/

2. Write the words that end with these sounds.

    a. /ch/   **b.** /ch/

    c. /ch/   **d.** /th/

3. Write **verse, verses,** and the picture words.

a.

b.

4. Use the words to write a sentence. Remember to use commas between the words in a list of things.

    purses   shirts   bought   .

    skirts   and   She   ,   ,

5. Write the word that means "to be on fire."
Then write the word with **ed.**

6. Write the word that means "look for."
Then write the word with **ing.**

Building Spelling Power

*We can add **er** to words to spell new words.*

rich—richer   poor—poorer

1. Add **er** to each of these words.

   a. soft   **b.** fast   **c.** low

   d. mean   **e.** great   **f.** old

2. Write Fern's question and the clerk's answer.

    the   purses   Where   are

    On   shelf   the   third

" ___?" asked Fern.

" ___," said the clerk.

Dictionary Help

/èr/ shows the vowel-r sounds in **her**, **first**, and **purse**.

94

Spelling Helps Reading

Sound out the /ėr/ words. Then read the story.

turn	germ	verb	clerk	firm	stir	third
chirp	snurk	bird	fern	first	girl	thirst
burp	curl	burst	curve	serve	sir	hurt

Mr. Burke had bought a large boat. He and his daughter Bert were showing it to a group of boys and girls in Bert's third grade class.

"I had to learn some boat terms," said Bert. "The back of the boat is a stern. Beds are berths. Those birds perched there are terns. Rough waves bursting on the sand are surf. The rising and falling seas are tides."

"Let us see how clever you are," said Mr. Burke. "See that rope ladder hanging from the side of the boat? Each rung is one foot from the next. The tide is touching the fourth rung now at noon. The tide rises one foot each hour. When will the tide rise to the first rung?"

"At three o'clock, of course, sir," cried Herb.

Was Herb right? Tell why or why not.
/ėr/ words? Snurks?

Test

95

sore
snore
score
corn
storm
born
north
sort
cork
warm
start
sharp
smart
warn
park
 world
 worse

19 More Sharp Thorns

More and *Thorn* words have the vowel-r

sounds in 🌵 .

We spell these vowel-r sounds **or** *or* **ore.**

Sharp words have the vowel-r

sounds in 💪 .

We spell these vowel-r sounds **ar.**

1. Say the six **ar** words. Write them.

2. Say the three **ore** words. Write them.

3. Say the six **or** words. Write them.
Circle the word that means "brought to life."

*Say **world** and **worse.***

*What vowel-r sounds do you hear in **world**?*

*What vowel-r sounds do you hear in **worse**?*

Why do we call these two words snurks?

4. Write **world, worse, more,** and **church.**
Circle the words that have the same
vowel-**r** sounds.

 Working with the Words

1. Write the picture words in alphabetical order.

sore

snore

score

corn

storm

born

north

sort

cork

warm

start

sharp

smart

warn

park

world

worse

2. Write the words that start with /w/.

3. Write the opposites of these words.

   a. dull   **b.** south

   c. cool   **d.** stop

4. Write the picture words.

   a. score or snore?

   b. sharp or smart?

   c. sore or sort?

   d. start or storm?

Building Spelling Power

1. Write **sort**. Change **s** to **p** and **f** to spell new words. Circle the word that means "a place for ships."

2. Write **cork**. Change **c** to **p** and **f** to spell new words. Circle the word that means "an eating tool."

3. Write **park**. Change **p** to **m** and **d** to spell new words. Circle the word that means "with no light."

4. Write **warm**. Change **w** to **h** and **f** to spell new words. Circle the word that means "hurt."

5. Write **forts** and **marks**. Circle the "doing word."

Dictionary Help

/ôr/ shows the vowel-r sounds in **more** and **horse**.
/är/ shows the vowel-r sounds in **smart**.

Sound out these vowel-r words. Then read the story.

chart	march	star	bark	arm	barn	art
bore	core	fork	tore	torch	pork	fort
chore	horse	shore	thorn	stork	worn	short
cord	porch	wore	sport	horn	store	more

"I am glad we gassed up and pumped up the tires, Art," said Mr. Archer. "We can drop off this load of corn at the store and still get some hard work done at the farm. See those dark clouds in the north? It may be warm, but I think a storm is coming up."

"I have some chores, too," said Art. "Stop, Dad! See that warning on the bridge crossing the road? LOW BRIDGE, 12 FEET."

"Our large truck is at least an inch higher than 12 feet! We cannot force our truck through!"

"There is no way to slip by! Park the truck, Dad. The cars in the back are starting to blow those horns at us."

"How in the world can we get by?" asked Mr. Archer.

"I have it," cried Art. "Come on, Dad! Let's......"

/ôr/ words?   /är/ words?

Test

20 Steer and Stare Words

fear
beard
spear
tear
deer
steer
peer
dare
spare
stare
fair
stairs
 heart
 tear
 wear

Steer words have the vowel-r sounds in . *We spell them with* **eer** *or* **ear.**

Stare words have the vowel-r sounds in . *We spell them with* **air** *or* **are.**

1. Write the **air** words. Draw a line under each **air.**
2. Write **dare** and the other words with **a-r-e.**

101

fear
beard
spear
tear
deer
steer
peer
dare
spare
stare
fair
stairs

3. Write the **ear** words that rhyme with

4. Write the **eer** words. Draw a line under each **eer.**

*Say **heart**. Why do we call **heart** a snurk?*

*Say the rhyming words **wear** and **tear.***

*Why are **wear** and **tear** snurks?*

5. Write the picture words. Circle the snurk.

a.

b.

c.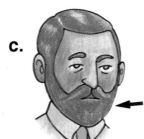

heart
tear
wear

6. Write the words that mean "pull in pieces" and "a drop of water from your eye."

1. Write the missing spelling words.

a.

a ____ tire

b.

a sharp ____

c.

a large ____

d.

curving ____

e.

a fat ____

f.

a torn ____

2. Each sentence has one wrong word.
Write the sentences right.

Our dog fairs storms. He does not

deer go out. He likes fear days.

Building Spelling Power

1. Write **fear.** Change **f** to **cl** and **r** to spell new words. Circle the word that means "back."

2. Write **deer.** Change **d** to **ch** and **sn** to spell new words. Circle the word that means "shout for joy."

3. Write **fair.** Change **f** to **p** and **ch** to spell new words. Circle the word that means "two of a kind."

4. Write **stare.** Change **st** to **b** and **sc** to spell new words. Circle the word that means "with no hair."

5. Add **ing** to **wear, tear,** and **cheer.**

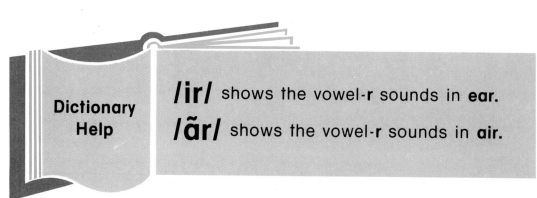

Dictionary Help

/ir/ shows the vowel-r sounds in **ear.**

/ãr/ shows the vowel-r sounds in **air.**

Sound out these vowel-r words. Then read the story.

share	rare	bare	ear	year	near
shear	snare	hair	jeer	rear	clear
scare	care	air	cheer	hear	dear

"Dad," cried Claire, "is that a hole in your sock? I dare say you tear up and wear out more than your fair share in one year! Why, you would go in your bare feet."

"Have a heart," groaned Mr. Ware, who was dozing in a chair near the fire. "I hear you! Cheer up and spare me your tears. Who cares? Who stares at my socks?"

"Mom and I do. Where are your clean socks?"

"Well, let us see how smart you are, Claire. In the drawer of my dresser I have six black and six brown socks all mixed up. I need a pair that match. Run up the stairs and get them. You may not turn on the lights, so you will not see which are black and which are brown. Now, Claire, what is the least number of socks you can bring down to be sure that you have a matching pair?"

What should Claire say?
Vowel-r words? Snurks?

Test

can't
didn't
isn't
I'm
it's
I'll
we'll
I'd
I've
let's
o'clock

won't
don't
couldn't
you're

21 It's Stuck

It's Stuck *words are* **contractions.**

A contraction is a word that is made by putting two or more words together and leaving out some of the letters.

We use an apostrophe to show where letters in a contraction are missing: **cannot** **can't**

1. Write the contractions for these words.

a. I will   **b.** I would   **c.** we will

2. Write the contractions for these words.

    a. did not   **b.** could not   **c.** is not

    d. I am   **e.** I have   **f.** you are

> Say **don't.** What vowel sound do you hear?
>
> Say **won't.** What vowel sound do you hear?
>
> Why do we call **don't** and **won't** snurks?

3. Write the contractions for these words.

    a. do not   **b.** let us   **c.** will not

4. Long ago people said, "It is ten of the clock."
Write **of the clock** and its contraction.

Working with the Words

1. Write the contractions for the opposites of
can, did, and **is.**

2. Write two words for each contraction.

a. you're   **b.** I've

c. I'll   **d.** isn't

e. didn't   **f.** let's

g. I'd   **h.** I'm

3. Write the sentences. Use contractions for **we will, it is,** and **could not.**

a.  **We will** go swimming if **it is** not too cool.

b. It **could not** go.

Building Spelling Power

Remember:

We use an apostrophe to show owning, too.

my friend's hat   a bear's tail

1. Write a contraction and an "owning word" for each sentence.

a.   The ___ shoes ___ fit her.

b.   They ___ fix the ___ front tire.

2. Write contractions for **could not** and **should not.**

3. Write contractions for **I have, you have, we have.**

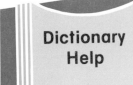

Dictionary Help   **/v/**   stands for the sound that ends **I've.**

109

Say these contractions. Then read the verse.

shouldn't	hasn't	he's	you'll	she's	we've
wouldn't	hadn't	he'll	they'll	he'd	you've
haven't	doesn't	she'll	they're	she'd	that's

Girl 1: Who thinks up ways for words to shrink?
Some printer who's run out of ink?
(I can't be sure—that's what I think.)

Boy 1: If I **will not,** I say "I **won't.**"
If I **do not,** I say "I **don't.**"
If I **could not,** I say "I **couldn't.**"
If I **should not,** I say "I **shouldn't.**"
(It works the same for **would** and
wouldn't.)

Girl 2: We've **can't** and **didn't, I'd** and **I'm.**
(The ink they'll save won't cost a dime.)
We say "**we'll** send" and then "**we've** sent."
I say "**I'll** go," but not "**I've** went."

Boy 2: And we'll not say "one **of the clock.**"
Let's shrink that down to "one **o'clock.**"
So when we shrink our words, you see,
It **is not (isn't)** done for free.

All: The price is one **a-pos-tro-phe.**

Test

22 Be-Bee Words

be	bee
meat	meet
blue	blew
road	rode
weak	week
made	maid
our	hour
deer	dear
sea	see
sew	so
son	sun
four	for
lead	led
weigh	way
your	you're

Be-Bee words are **homonyms**.

Homonyms are words that sound alike but have different spellings and different meanings.

to—too—two	be—bee
/tü/	/bē/

 1. Write ![4], ![sun], and ![cloud], and their homonyms.

111

be	*bee*
sew	*so*
meat	*meet*
your	*you're*
blue	*blew*
road	*rode*
son	*sun*
weak	*week*
made	*maid*
four	*for*
lead	*led*
weigh	*way*
our	*hour*
deer	*dear*
sea	*see*

2. Write the picture words first. Then write their homonyms.

a.

b.

c.

d.

e.

f.

3. Write the words for "seven days," "one o'clock to two o'clock," and "you are." Then write the homonyms.

112

4. Write the words that mean "stitch," "showed the way," and "look at." Then write the homonyms.

Working with the Words

1. Use five words to write a sentence.

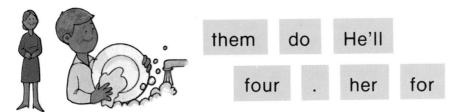

them   do   He'll

four   .   her   for

2. Use five words to write a sentence.

dear   .   for   friend

deer   It's   her

3. Use four words to write a sentence.

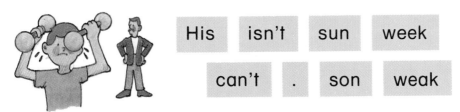

His   isn't   sun   week

can't   .   son   weak

Building Spelling Power

1. Add **ing** to each verb: **sew, see, be.**

2. Write the missing spelling words.

a.

They **ride** now.

They ___ then.

b.

The wind **blows.**

It ___ for an hour.

c.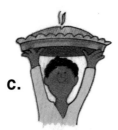

He can **make** a pie.

He ___ a big pie.

3. Write "describing words" for these meanings.

   a. much loved   **b.** not strong   **c.** with no hair

Dictionary Help   **/y/** shows the sound that starts **your** and **you're.**

Spelling Helps Reading

Say these homonyms. Then read the story.

to	too	two	know	no	there	their
buy	by		red	read	one	won
write	right		hear	here	new	knew
			would	wood		

"Let's play that word game we thought up," said Ann. "We use spelling words and words in the Spelling Helps Reading list in sentences. The one who uses the most words from the two lists wins. Who has a sentence?"

"I'll start," said Dick. "I've used two words from the lists: **He knew he had read the book.**"

"I can beat that," cried Jane. "I use three words: **This meat will not stay fresh for more than an hour.**"

"I've got five in mine," said Paul. "This is it: **We'll buy two new blue suits next week.**"

"I have two more than you do, Paul," said Madge. "Hear this one: **No one will know the right place to meet if we don't write it down.**"

Can you write a sentence with more words from the Be-Bee lists than Madge used?

Test

115

cent	sent
sail	sale
tail	tale
pail	pale
stare	stair
heel	heal

23 Bare-Bear Words

bear	bare
weight	wait
break	brake
through	threw
fourth	forth
heard	herd
eight	ate
whole	hole
rein	rain

Bare-Bear words are homonyms.

Homonyms sound alike but have different spellings and meanings.

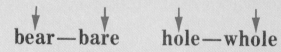

bear—bare   hole—whole

/bãr/   /hōl/

1. Write the two /ãr/ homonym pairs.

    a. /ãr/   **b.** /ãr/

Sound-spellings show how we say words.
/brāk/ shows every sound in **break** and **brake.**

2. Write the homonym pairs for the sound-spellings.

a. /hėrd/   **b.** /hōl/   **c.** /fôrth/

d. /rān/   **e.** /wāt/   **f.** /brāk/

3. Write the picture words. Then write their homonyms.

  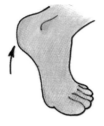

a.   b.   c.

4. Write and five words that rhyme with   .

Circle the word that means "not bright."

117

Working with the Words

bear	*bare*
weight	*wait*
break	*brake*
through	*threw*
fourth	*forth*
cent	*sent*
sail	*sale*
heard	*herd*
tail	*tale*
pail	*pale*
eight	*ate*
stare	*stair*
whole	*hole*
heel	*heal*
rein	*rain*

1. Write the homonym pairs for these sound-spellings.

   a. /thrü/   **b.** /stãr/   **c.** /hėrd/

2. Write the words /fôrth/ and /hōl/ for the sentence.

   The mouse crept ___ from its ___ .

3. Write the words /hōl/ and /pāl/ for the sentence.

   She has a ___ ___ of fresh milk.

118

Building Spelling Power

The first verb in each pair tells what we do "now." The second verb in each pair tells what we did "in the past."

think — thought   **bring — brought**

Write the missing "in the past" verbs.

1. hear   **2.** send

3. throw   **4.** blow

5. eat   **6.** ride

7. buy   **8.** make

9. sell   **10.** draw

11. sink   **12.** break

13. meet   **14.** tell

Dictionary Help

/w/ shows the sound that starts **wait** and **weight.**

/h/ shows the sound that starts **herd** and **heard.**

Say these homonym snurks. Then read the story.

to	one	their	son	through	weigh
two	won	there	sew	whole	weight
buy	here	your	break	rein	four
would	fourth	you're	heard	eight	bear

"Let's play the word game once more," said Jack. "This time we'll use all the homonyms we've had."

The class got to work. Mike O'Hare raised his hand.

"I used three: He threw his weight on the brake."

"I have three, too," said Madge. "The stag led the herd of deer."

"I used four," said Fern. "No one found the right way."

"I used five," said Fred. "Did you know there is a big one cent sale?"

"I didn't count mine," said Kate, "but I think I'll win. This is mine: I would like to buy four new blue pens for our dear friends to write with."

How many homonyms did Kate use in her sentence? Can you write one with more? Try.

24 Knock-Knee Words

knife
knock
knee
wrong
wrap
wrist
crumb
thumb
chalk
taught
fright

sign
comb
half
calf

Knock-Knee words have silent consonant letters.

knee /nē/   **wrap** /rap/   **crumb** /krum/

fright /frīt/   **chalk** /chôk/   **half** /haf/

1. Write the words with silent **k** before **n**.
2. Write the words with silent **w** before **r**.

3. Write the words that end with silent **b.**

4. Write **sign** and the words with silent **gh.**

5. Write the words with silent **l.** Circle the snurks.

 Working with the Words

1. Write the picture words.

a.    b.    c.

d.    e. 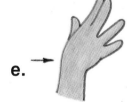   f.

2. Write the words that start with the /k/ sound in alphabetical order.

3. Write the word for each meaning.

a. not right   **b.** rap

c. a scare   **d.** a small bit

Say **pond, clock,** and **comb.**

Why do we call **comb** a snurk?

Say **silk, since,** and **sign.**

Why do we call **sign** a snurk?

4. Write the snurks.
Draw lines under the /a/ words.

knife
knock
knee
wrong
wrap
wrist
crumb
thumb
chalk
taught
fright
sign
comb
half
calf

5. Write the sentence using two of these words.

have   half   hole   whole

A ___ peach is more than ___ of a peach.

123

Building Spelling Power

Write the sentences.

1.
climb . to limb

Don't up high that

2.
come tight won't

This loose . knot

3.
walk the . through

snow couldn't John

Dictionary Help

/m/ stands for the sound that starts **made**.
/m/ stands for the sound that ends **thumb**.

124

Spelling Helps Reading

Read the words.

climb	should	knot	light	write	wrote	whose
could	kneel	know	night	talk	who	straight
eight	knew	lamb	right	walk	whole	weight

Find a word in each row that does not fit.
Nouns go with nouns, verbs with verbs.

1. climb   kneel   knit   (dumb)   know
2. taught   two   caught   fought   wrote
3. knelt   knew   straight   thought   slept
4. knot   lamb   night   weight   kneel
5. knife   wreath   tight   crumb   wrist
6. thumb   calf   chalk   bought   sign
7. knee   limb   high   wrench   plumber
8. knob   wren   bright   wringer   knives

Put **g** and **h** in **through** and **right**
And **w** in **wrong** and **write**.
A **lamb** may **kneel** down on its **knees**,
So don't leave out those **k**'s and **b**'s.
A **calf** can **walk**. Don't sound the **l**.
But do not skip it when you spell.

Test

dir ty
emp ty
sil ly
sor ry
ug ly
cra zy
ea sy
ti ny
ang ry
hung ry
∇ on ly
∇ bus y
∇ eve ry
∇ ear ly
∇ heav y

25 Very Ugly Words

Very Ugly words have two parts, or syllables.

*In **Very Ugly** words, the y at the end spells /ē/.*

 1. Write the words in which the last syllable is **ly**.

2. Write the words in which the last syllable is <u>not</u> **ly**.

126

Say every. Hear the two syllables.
The word every looks like a three-part word,
but the e in the middle is silent.

/ev′ rē/

3. Write **heavy, ugly,** and **every.**
Circle the word that means "weighing a lot."

We hear the /ng/ sound in the first syllable
of angry and hungry.
We hear the /g/ sound in the second syllable.
But we see only one letter g.

angry   /ang′ grē/

4. Write **angry** and **hungry.**
Circle the word that means "wanting food."

Working with the Words

1. Write the word for each meaning.

    a. very small   **b.** not clean   **c.** not pretty

dirty

empty

silly

sorry

ugly

crazy

easy

tiny

angry

hungry

only

busy

every

early

heavy

2. Write the word for each meaning.

a. hard at work   **b.** just one

c. not hard   **d.** not late

> The Very Ugly words tell how things look or feel. They are **adjectives,** or "describing words."

3. Write the picture adjectives.

a.    **b.**

c.    **d.**

4. The sentence has three mistakes. Write it right.

   every cat has a crasy hat

Building Spelling Power

Say the Very Ugly words. In each word the first syllable is loud and the second syllable is soft. An accent mark shows the loud syllable.

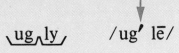

/ug′ lē/

Write the missing words. The sound-spellings tell you which words to write.

1.  He's ___ he acted ___.

   /sôr′ ē/   /sil′ ē/

2.  Her ___ book is ___.

   /tī′ nē/   /ē′ zē/

3.  ___ dog was ___.

   /ev′ rē/   /hung′ grē/

Dictionary Help   /z/ shows the sound in **crazy**.

Sound out these words. Then read the story.

fancy	safety	jolly	icy	salty	loudly
truly	baby	simply	noisy	nearly	greasy
plenty	curly	thirsty	hardly	barely	slowly

"Have a busy day at the store, Daddy?" asked Nancy Hardy. "You're home early."

"Hardly," said Mr. Hardy slowly. "I'm very angry. I had a dirty trick played on me, I'm sorry to say. A big husky man bought a pair of heavy work shoes for $12. He handed me a greasy $20 bill. I had no change. Wally Tracy in the candy store had plenty. He gave me twenty $1 bills. I gave the man eight $1 bills in change. The $20 bill was no good. I paid Tracy back. I'm out the $12 shoes, $8 in change, and the $20 I paid Tracy."

"You lost $40?" cried Mrs. Hardy. "Not funny!"

"No, Betsy. I gave $8 to the man and $20 to Tracy. So I'm out only $28."

"You're both wrong," said Nancy. "You really lost . . . ."

How many **y**-ending words in the story?

Test

130

26 Puppy-Puppies

can dy	can dies
cit y	cit ies
pup py	pup pies
po ny	po nies
bod y	bod ies
dair y	dair ies
cook y	cook ies
ar my	ar mies
jel ly	jel lies
cop y	cop ies
hob by	hob bies
pen ny	pen nies
wor ry	wor ries
cher ry	cher ries
coun try	coun tries

*When words end in a consonant letter and **y**, we change the **y** to **i** before adding **es**.*

1. Write the **y**-ending words that start with /p/.
Below each word, write its **ies** form.

candies
cities
puppies
ponies
bodies
dairies
cookies
armies
jellies
copies
hobbies
pennies

worries
cherries
countries

2. Write the **ies** words that start with /k/.

3. Write the **ies** forms of **hobby, jelly, dairy,** and **army.**

4. Write the **y**-ending forms of **cities, bodies,** and **pennies.** Circle the word for "a cent."

We use

    or to spell the /ôr/ sound in fork,

    er to spell the /èr/ sound in her,

    ou to spell the /ou/ sound in out.

*Say **worry, cherry,** and **country.***

Why do we call these words snurks?

5. Write and .

Circle the snurk.

6. Write the **y**-ending forms of the snurks.
Circle the word that names a place.

Working with the Words

1. Write the picture words. Draw a line
under the first syllable in each word.

a.

b.

c.

d.

e.

f.

2. Write the spelling words that belong in the
sentences.

a. He has
many ___.

b. She makes
jelly ___.

c. This is
cherry ___.

Building Spelling Power

Remember: An accent mark shows the loud syllable.

\pup˄py/   \pup'˄ē/

Write the words for which you see the sound-spellings.

1.
He's in the ___ of his ___.

/är' mē/   /kun' trē/

2.
There's one ___ in the ___.

/dãr' ē/   /sit' ē/

3.
The ___ pulls a ___.

/pō' nē/   /bug' ē/

Dictionary Help

/j/ shows the sound that starts **jelly** and **jellies.**

 # Spelling Helps Reading

Sound out these words. Then read the verse.

story — stories	party — parties	county — counties
navy — navies	buggy — buggies	bunny — bunnies
daisy — daisies	thirty — thirties	twenty — twenties

All: If you have nouns that end with **y**
That you would like to mul-ti-ply,
You will get more, and never less.
Just change the **y** to **i-e-s.**

Boys: Tell your stories, feed your puppies,

Girls: Ride your ponies, catch some guppies,

Boys: Go to parties, read the funnies,

Girls: Make some copies, pat your bunnies,

Boy 1: Bake your cookies, pick your cherries,
Eat your candies, cook your berries.

Girl 1: We get milk from cows in dairies,
Dimes and quarters from tooth fairies.

All: So tack **e-s** onto your penny
And you'll have not just one, but many.
Drop them in your piggy banks,
And when you're rich, send us your thanks!

Test

bet ter
sis ter
but ter
cor ner
let ter
flow er
col lar
cel lar
sail or
mir ror
neigh bor
sug ar
an swer
broth er
an oth er

27 Better Sailor Collar

In **Better Sailor Collar** words, the soft syllable ends with a vowel letter and **r**.

er spells the vowel-**r** sounds in **better**.
or spells the vowel-**r** sounds in **sailor**.
ar spells the vowel-**r** sounds in **collar**.

1. Write the words with the **er** ending. Circle the snurks.

136

2. Write the words with **ar** endings. Circle the snurk.

3. Write the words with **or** endings. Circle the snurks.

4. Write **brother, another,** and **answer.**

5. Write **letter, sugar,** and **sister** in alphabetical order.

Working with the Words

1. Write the picture words.

a.

b.

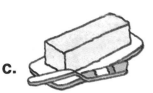

c.

2. Write the words for "more than one flower" and "more than one mirror."

better
sister
butter
corner
letter
flower
collar
cellar
sailor

▽S

mirror
neighbor
sugar
answer
brother
another

The snurks have tricky spellings.
Tell why they are snurks.

3. Write the snurks with these sounds in the loud syllables.

   a. /ā/   **b.** /sh/

   c. /a/   **d.** /ir/

4. Each sentence has a wrong word. Use spelling words in place of the wrong words. Write the sentences right.

a.    Mother adds salt to make food sweet.

b.    My brother likes better on his bread.

138

Building Spelling Power

1. Add **or** to **sail, tail,** and **tract** to spell new words.

a.    b.    c.

2. Add **er** to **teach, check,** and **sweep** to spell new words.

a.    b.    c.

3. Write the missing words.

a.    The two ___ are

playing ___.

b.    The ___ is showing

the class a ___.

Dictionary Help   /ŦH/ shows the sound in **brother.**

Spelling Helps Reading

Sound out these words.

under	beggar	cedar	clever	farmer	tower
ever	whisper	tailor	dinner	harbor	paper
actor	author	silver	winter	doctor	tractor

Choose the right words for the sentences.

1. Winter is to **summer** as **younger** is to...

        faster   clever   (older)

2. Father is to **son** as **mother** is to...

        sister   daughter   brother

3. Tailor is to **needle** as **farmer** is to...

        tractor   quarter   banner

4. Nearer is to **farther** as **better** is to...

        worse   good   silver

5. Author is to **writer** as **pastor** is to...

        painter   preacher   beggar

6. Cedar is to **tree** as **rose** is to...

        flower   clover   flavor

Vowel-R spellings! Picky, picky!
E-R, O-R, A-R —— Tricky!

Test

140

28 Little Turtle

lit tle
bot tle
bub ble
ta ble
can dle
mid dle
tur tle
han dle
nee dle
a ble
ap ple
un cle
whis tle
▽ peo ple
▽ trou ble

In each Little Turtle word,
the soft syllable ends with **le.**

1. Write the words with double consonant letters.
Draw a line under each soft syllable.

2. Write the words with **n d** and **r t.**
Draw a line under each soft syllable.

little
bottle
bubble
table
candle
middle
turtle
handle
needle
able
apple
uncle
whistle

S

people
trouble

3. Write  and the word that rhymes with .

4. Write 🕯 and the word that rhymes with 🕯.

5. Write **uncle, needle,** and **whistle.** Circle the word with a silent **t.**

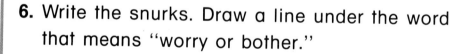

*Say **people** and **trouble.***

*Do we expect **eo** to spell /ē/?*

*Do we expect **ou** to spell /u/?*

*Why do we call **people** and **trouble** snurks?*

6. Write the snurks. Draw a line under the word that means "worry or bother."

7. Write the picture words.

a.    **b.**

142

Working with the Words

1. Add **s** to Little Turtle words to spell "more than one."

a.

b.

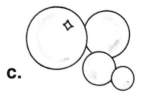

c.

d.

e.

f.

2. Three spelling words have the /i/ sound in the loud syllable. Write the /i/ words in alphabetical order.

3. The letters in these words are mixed up.
Spell the words.

   a. labe   **b.** cunel   **c.** poleep

   d. tebal   **e.** papel   **f.** dimdel

Building Spelling Power

Nouns are "naming words."

Nouns name people or places or things.

brother	country	needle
sister	city	sugar

1. Write **le**-ending nouns with doubled consonants.

a.    b.    c.

Adjectives are "describing words."

Adjectives tell how things look or sound.

little child   **busy** people   **purple** cloth

2. Write **simple, little, nibble, bundle,** and **gentle.**
Draw a line under each adjective.

Dictionary Help

/n/ shows the sound that starts **needle.**

Sound out these words. Then read the story.

ankle	circle	paddle	steeple	gobble	juggle
bundle	eagle	pickle	sparkle	simple	settle
cattle	gentle	wrinkle	puzzle	saddle	jungle

"It's simple, Billy," said Uncle Ben. "Mark a little circle on the maple tree. Whittle a hole and plug in a spout. Loop the handles over the spout. The sap trickles into the pail. People bottle the sap and pour it on griddle cakes and waffles. We boil it, too, to make sugar. Here, have a sample."

Uncle Ben dipped a ladle into one of the pails. Billy's eyes sparkled as he tasted the sweet sap.

"Now, Billy," chuckled Uncle Ben, "you can barely reach those pails. The trees grow at least one foot each year. Next year you won't be able to reach the pails."

Billy looked puzzled. Then his eyes twinkled.

"Yes, I will. I'll be able to reach them every year!"

Why will Billy be able to reach the pails?

Don't get in trouble when you spell.
The **l-e** sounds just like **e-l**.

Test

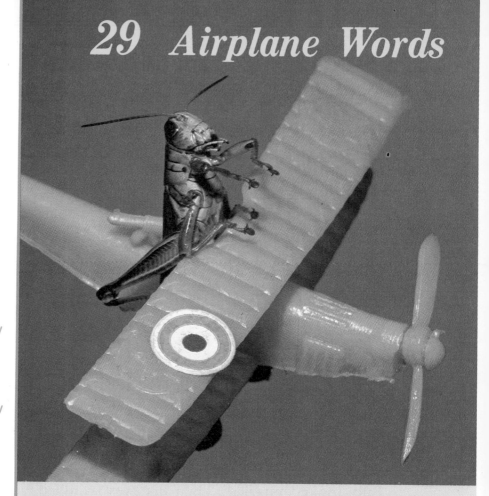

29 Airplane Words

in side
out side
can not
for got
be side
be long
may be
air plane
with out
side walk
good-by
in to
to day
no thing
in stead

Airplane words are called **compound** words. We make compound words by putting short words together.

$$air + plane = airplane$$

We learn to spell compound words by seeing the short words and spelling them.

 1. Write the compounds with **side.**

2. Write the compounds with **be** as one of the short words. Circle the word that means "by the side of."

3. Put short words together to form compounds.

a. can not   **b.** air plane   **c.** in to

d. for got   **e.** to day   **f.** with out

*Say **no** and **thing**. Then say **nothing**.*

*Why do we call **nothing** a snurk?*

*Why do we call **into, today,** and **instead** snurks?*

4. Write **good-by, nothing,** and **instead.** Circle the compound that has a **hyphen,** or small line, between the shorter words.

Working with the Words

1. Write **inside** and the word that means "not inside."

inside
outside
cannot
forgot
beside
belong
maybe
airplane
without
sidewalk
good-by

S

into
today
nothing
instead

2. Write the word you say when you go away.

3. Use the words to tell what the boy said.

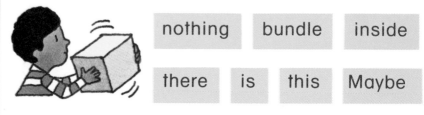

nothing	bundle	inside
there	is	this	Maybe

Peter said, "___."

4. Write the words for the spaces. The sound-spellings tell you which words to write.

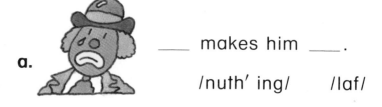

a. ___ makes him ___.

/nuth' ing/   /laf/

b. They ___ ___ to him.

/bōth/   /bē lông'/

148

Building Spelling Power

1. Spell the new compound words.

a.

b.

c.

d.

e.

f.

2. Use the words in each box to spell two compound words.

a.
base	air
plane	ball

b.
side	out
with	walk

Dictionary Help

/tü/ shows how we say **to**.

/dā/ shows how we say **day**.

/tü dā'/ shows how we say **today**.

Sound out these compound words.

baseball	cowboy	handlebars	stepladder
butterflies	fingernail	horseshoes	tablecloth
buttermilk	flowerpot	rainbow	pancake
candlestick	football	sailboat	waterfall

Choose the words that do not belong. Tell why.

1. woodpecker   bluebird   peacock   reindeer
2. eyebrow   toothbrush   eardrum   kneecap
3. bookcase   fireplace   flashlight   footstool
4. snowsuit   raincoat   earmuffs   bathrobe
5. butterfly   cockroach   sunfish   bumblebee
6. peanuts   popcorn   cheesecake   toothpaste
7. flagpole   fishhook   stickpin   thumbtack
8. redwing   greenhouse   bobwhite   sidewalk

Sing a song of sixpence, have a ham on rye —
Blackberry, blueberry, huckleberry pie!
You will have no trouble, if you play it smart —
Spot the compound pieces and spell them part by part!

Test

150

30 Breakfast Words

her self
him self
my self

some one
some time
every one
break fast
any thing
some thing
every thing
grand father
grand mother
to morrow
any one
your self

Breakfast words are compound words.

We put two shorter words together to form compound words.

We learn to spell compound words by seeing the shorter words and spelling first one and then the other.

break + fast = breakfast

1. Say the Breakfast words.
Write the compounds with **some** or **self**.

herself
himself
myself

someone
sometime
everyone
breakfast
anything
something
everything
grandfather
grandmother
tomorrow
anyone
yourself

2. Write the compounds with
any or **every.**

3. Write compounds with
grand, fast, or **to.**

Many compound words have snurk
parts you have learned. Read the
different snurk parts in the list.

4. Write the nine snurk parts that are
in the compound words.

5. Write the picture compounds.

a.

b.

Working with the Words

1. Write the compound words with these meanings.

   a. morning meal   **b.** day after today   **c.** I or me

> We use a **comma** between **Yes** or **No** and the rest of a sentence.
>
> Yes, I'll do it myself.
>
> No, I don't want anything.

2. Use the words to write the Yes and No sentences.

a.

| to | going | Grandmother's |

| house | I'm | tomorrow |

Yes, ___ .

b.

| his | hasn't | had |

| Grandfather | breakfast |

No, ___ .

Building Spelling Power

Use **er-** or **le**-ending words in these compounds.

1.  *flowerpot*

2.

3.

4.

5.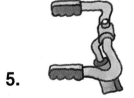

6.

7.

8.

Dictionary Help

What compound does this show?

/ev′ rē hwãr/

154

Spelling Helps Reading

Sound out these compound words.

yesterday	toothbrush	birdhouse	peanut
overcoat	cardboard	newspaper	mailbox
haircut	footprints	flashlight	airport
bedroom	anybody	eyebrow	flagpole

Write **T** for **True** or **F** for **False**. Tell why you think so.

1. Everything in a newspaper headline is true.

2. Everyone is bound to do something wrong sometime.

3. Many people buy peanuts and popcorn at baseball games.

4. Football fans sometimes need waterproof raincoats.

5. We buy lawnmowers at hardware stores.

6. Chalkboards are useful in classrooms.

7. Everyone likes to eat grapefruit at breakfast.

8. Mailboxes make good birdhouses for bluejays.

9. Airplanes need runways to land at airports.

10. Farmers use pitchforks to make haystacks.

How many compounds are in the sentences?

Test

bot tom
hel lo
bor row
but ton
fol low
squir rel
writ ten
bal loon
rab bit
kit ten
hap pen
les son
yel low
sup pose
sud den

31 Hello Rabbit

Hello Rabbit words are two-syllable words with double consonant letters.

↓ ↓
hello **rabbit**

*We divide **Hello Rabbit** words into syllables between the double consonant letters.*

↓ ↓
hel lo **rab bit**

1. Write the words with double **t** or double **p**.
Draw a line under the first syllable in each word.

156

2. Write the words with double **r**, double **b**, or double **d**. Draw a line under the first syllable in each.

3. Write the words with double **l** or double **s**. Draw a line under the first syllable in each word.

4. Write the words and say them. Draw a line under each loud syllable.

    a. It can pop.   **b.** "Hi!"   **c.** It eats nuts.

Working with the Words

1. Write the picture words.

a.

b.

c.

bottom
hello
borrow
button
follow
squirrel
written
balloon
rabbit
kitten
happen
lesson
yellow
suppose
sudden

2. Write the words that start like .

3. Write the words that start like .

Two-syllable words are easy to spell if we look at each syllable and spell the words by parts.

Say rabbit. See **rab bit** .

Spell **rab** *like a Fat Cat word.*

Spell **bit** *like a Big Pig word.*

4. Write the words with these first syllables.

    a. yel   **b.** les

    c. kit   **d.** fol

Building Spelling Power

Find mistakes in the sentences. Write them right.

1. Rabbits clime tree,

2. Yellow, brown green, and purpel are collars.

3. Baloons are sometimes filled with ear?

4. "Hello," Said Betty. "Im glad to meat you."

Spelling Helps Reading

Sound out the words. Then read the story.

allow	traffic	arrow	attack	ribbon	tennis
swallow	collect	coffee	pillow	hidden	common
appear	hammer	inning	correct	narrow	quarrel

On Saturday afternoon, Mr. Dutton was napping in his hammock in the late summer sun.

"Daddy," said Ellen, "aren't you going to paint my puppy's kennel?"

"Hello, Ellen," said her father, rubbing his eyes. "I suppose I can do it tomorrow. I'll be out of town all next week. You and Jimmy had better hurry and get the paint. Hammond's hardware store closes at six. Get a gallon of green. Run so you'll be back for dinner. Watch for traffic!"

"Sorry, young fellow," said Mr. Hammond to Jimmy. "It happens that I'm out of green. Got red, blue, and yellow, by the gallon and half gallon. No green, though."

"Oh, Jimmy," cried Ellen, "what can we do?"

"Don't worry, Sis," said Jimmy with a smile. "You'll have a bright green kennel by Sunday night. I'll just...."

Hello Rabbit words?

Test

32 Picnic Basket

pic nic
pen cil
un til
bas ket
win dow
en joy
al so
gar den
ex pect
al ways
cir cus
in vite
mar ket
mon key
al most

Picnic Basket words are two-syllable words with the Vowel-Consonant-Consonant-Vowel letter pattern.

pic nic **bas ket**

VC CV VC CV

We divide **Picnic Basket** *words between the two consonants.*

1. Write the words that start with vowel letters.
Draw a line under the first syllable in each word.

161

picnic
pencil
until
basket
window
enjoy
also
garden
expect
always
circus
invite
market

monkey
almost

2. Write the words that start with consonants.
Circle the snurk.

> Say **monkey.** Hear the vowel sounds.
>
> Do we expect **o** to spell /u/?
>
> Why do we call **monkey** a snurk?

3. Write **window** and **monkey.**
Circle the word with the /ng/ sound.

4. Write **picnic, circus,** and **almost.**
Circle the word with two /s/ sounds.

5. Write the picture words.

a.

b.

Working with the Words

1. Write the words for these meanings.

    a. too   **b.** be happy with   **c.** all the time

Spell two-syllable words by parts.

  *Say **garden**.   See* ＼gar＾den／*.*
  *Spell **gar** like a Smart word.*
  *Spell **den** like a Red Hen word.*

2. Write the words with these first syllables.

    a. bas   **b.** cir

    c. pen   **d.** pic

    e. in   **f.** win

3. Write the three words that start with /ô/.

4. The letter **x** spells the /ks/ sounds. Write the word with the letter **x.** Write the **ing** and **ed** forms also.

Building Spelling Power

Find the mistakes and write the sentences right.

1. They have gone two the Circus.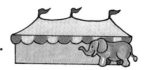

2. We expect to plant a garden in our back yarn,

3. always put your pencil in you're desk.

4. Do you enjoy looking out off the window.

Dictionary Help

/ks/ shows the sounds **x** spells in **expect.**

/eks pekt′/ is how we say **expect.**

Spelling Helps Reading

Sound out these ‿VC‿CV‿ words. Then read the story.

contest	napkin	invent	turkey	signal	servant
turnip	husband	absent	perfect	master	problem
certain	mistake	thunder	platform	person	perhaps

"Perhaps your mother would enjoy perfume," said Mr. Lambert. "It makes a splendid birthday gift. A person seldom makes a mistake with perfume."

"That's a perfect answer to our problem, Arlene," said Norman. "How much, Mr. Lambert?"

"With the velvet box, it costs ten dollars. Tell you what I'll do. After Mrs. Denton uses up the perfume, bring me the bottle. I always show lovely bottles in my store window. I'll pay back the cost of the bottle. The perfume costs nine dollars more than the bottle."

"You mean we collect a dollar for the empty bottle?"

"That's not correct, Norman," laughed Arlene. "You need a number lesson."

Was Norman right? How much will Mr. Lambert pay?
‿VC‿CV‿ words? Snurks?

Test

165

a|bout
a|round
a|larm
a|like
a|way
a|live
a|go
a|wake
a|part
a|long
a|lone

a|head
a|gain
a|bove
a|mong

33 About Alike Words

About Alike words are two-syllable words with the **Vowel-Consonant-Vowel** letter pattern.

a|bout   a|like   a|part

V|CV   V|CV   V|CV

About Alike words divide before the consonant.

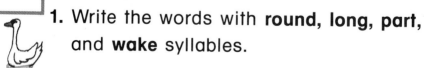

1. Write the words with **round, long, part,** and **wake** syllables.

2. Write the words with /ō/ in the second syllable.

166

3. Write the words for these meanings.
Draw a line under the second syllable
in each word.

a. the same   **b.** not sleeping   **c.** not dead

d. gone   **e.** once more   **f.** higher than

Do **ea** and **ia** usually spell /e/ as they do

in **ahead** and **again?**

Do **o**-consonant letter-**e** and **o** usually spell

/u/ as they do in **above** and **among?**

Why do we call these words snurks?

4. Write the snurks. Circle the snurk syllables.

5. Write **alarm, about,** and **ago** in alphabetical order.

6. Write **among, apart, around,** and **alone** in
alphabetical order.

Working with the Words

about
around
alarm
alike
away
alive
ago
awake
apart
along
alone

ahead
again
above
among

Write a spelling word for each space.

1. They're ____.

2. It's an ____.

3. He's not ____.

4. It was long ____.

5. It goes ____.

6. It's ____ cats.

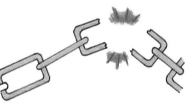

7. It came ____.

8. He ran ____.

Building Spelling Power

1. Use each of these words as a second syllable
to write six About Alike words.

while	woke	loud	side	rise	mount

2. Write the sentences. Use the periods and commas.

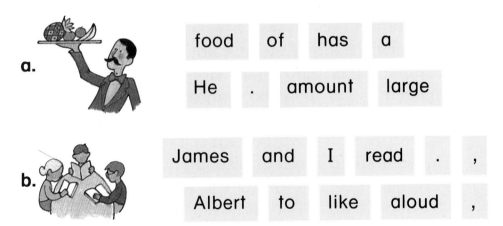

a.

food	of	has	a

He	.	amount	large

b.

James	and	I	read	.	,

Albert	to	like	aloud	,

Dictionary Help

/ī/ shows how we say **eye** and I.
We do not use capitals
in sound-spelling.

Spelling Helps Reading

Sound out the ‿V‿CV‿ words. Then read the story.

awoke	adult	amuse	award	ajar	amaze
avoid	adore	aside	ashore	adopt	arose
arise	aloud	awhile	amount	aboard	await

When Homer awoke, he arose and dressed. It was his birthday! Homer knew his gift from Grandfather Davis would be there. Grandfather lived in another state, far away. Homer had not seen him since he was a year old, long ago. Grandfather alone always knew what Homer wanted. Again and again Homer had been amazed to get what he wanted. This year, above all, Homer wanted a first base mitt.

And there on the breakfast table lay his gifts! Homer looked around among them for his grandfather's gift. He took it aside and opened it.

There it was! The mitt! But Homer's yell of delight turned into a groan when he tried it on.

"Don't be alarmed, Homer," said his dad. "We can get another one. Grandfather had no way of knowing."

What was the matter with the mitt?

‿V‿CV‿ words? Snurks?

Test

34 Parade Music

pa rade
be hind
bro ken
mu sic
e ven
cho sen
be cause
o pen
de cide
rea son
de serve
be fore
re turn
po lite
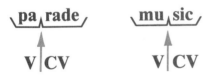 be come

Parade Music words are two-syllable words that have the Vowel-Consonant-Vowel letter pattern.

pa rade   **mu sic**

V | C V   V | C V

We divide Parade Music words before the consonant.

1. Write the words with the **be** syllable.
Circle the snurk.

parade
behind
broken
music
even
chosen
because
open
decide
reason
deserve
before
return
polite

become

In some Parade Music words, the first syllable is loud. In some Parade Music words, the second syllable is loud. **The accent mark** shows the loud syllable.

be₍hind′   rea′₍son   po₍lite′

2. Write **parade, even,** and **reason.**
   Mark the loud syllables.

3. Write **decide, deserve,** and **music.**
   Mark the loud syllables.

4. Write **chosen, broken, polite,** and **open.**
   Circle the words with a loud first syllable.

5. Write **return** and its **ing** form.

Working with the Words

\V\CV\ words are easy to spell if we spell the words by parts.

Say behind.   See \be\hind\.

Spell be as you spell me and we and he.
Spell hind as you spell find and mind.

1. Write the words with these loud syllables.

    a. bro′   **b.** cho′

    c. o′   **d.** rea′

    e. e′   **f.** mu′

2. Write **shut** and the word that means "not shut."

3. Write an adjective for each picture.

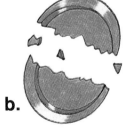

  a.   **b.**   **c.**

173

Building Spelling Power

1. Add **ly** to **even** and **polite** to spell more words.

2. Find the mistakes in the sentences.
Write the sentences right.

a. Tommys painting was chosen as the beast.

b. The drummer's are marking in a parad.

c. we have decided too move before
winter begin.

Dictionary Help

Read this:

/bē kum′/ /iz/ /ā/ /snėrk/.

Spelling Helps Reading

Sound out these ‿V‿CV‿ words. Then read the story.

began	protest	beneath	pilot	prepare	repair
direct	silent	final	spider	season	stolen
moment	below	motel	stupid	reward	pretend

The pupils in Edith Mason's room decided to spend recess time telling riddles. Edith was chosen to begin.

"Here's my riddle," she said. "Pretend that the school band is playing music in a parade before a football game. Students who play the drums march in a group. One drummer marches ahead of two drummers. One drummer marches between two drummers. Finally, one drummer marches politely behind two drummers. What is the least number of drummers that belong in the band?"

The pupils were silent for a moment.

"There were nine drummers," cried David.

"No, there were five," said Suzy Dolan.

Who was right? How many drummers were there? How many ‿V‿CV‿ words? Snurks?

Test

175.

seven
second
present
finish
wag on
met al
vis it
pun ish
trav el
or ange
giv en
shad ow
min ute
prom ise

money

Travel Wagon words are two-syllable words with the VC V letter pattern.

sev en | min ute | vis it

VC|V | VC|V | VC|V

We divide Travel Wagon words after the consonant.

1. Write the words that start with /m/.
Circle the snurk.

2. Write the words that start with /s/.

176

3. Write the words that start with /p/ and with /t/.

4. Write the spelling words with these
vowel sounds in the first syllable.

    a. /i/   **b.** /i/   **c.** /i/

    d. /i/   **e.** /o/   **f.** /e/

    g. /e/   **h.** /e/   **i.** /e/

5. Write the picture words.

a.    **b.**    **c.**

d.   **e.**    **f.**

Working with the Words

seven
second
present
finish
wagon
metal
visit
punish
travel
orange
given
shadow
minute
promise

money

1. Write the "more than one" picture words.

a.

b.

2. Write the words for these meanings.

a. six plus one

b. next after first

c. end

d. gift

3. The syllables in ⟍vis⟍el⟋ and ⟍trav⟍it⟋ are mixed up.
The words should be **visit** and **travel**.

Write these mixed up words right:

⟍or⟍ise⟋   ⟍prom⟍ange⟋

4. Write the snurks in this question:
Does your father have any money
to give you?

Building Spelling Power

1. Write the **ing** forms of **promise, finish,** and **punish.**

2. Write the sentences.

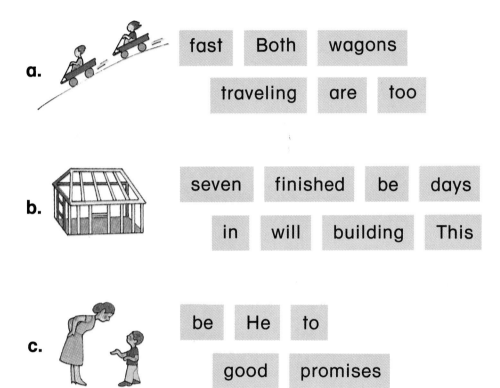

a. fast   Both   wagons   traveling   are   too

b. seven   finished   be   days   in   will   building   This

c. be   He   to   good   promises

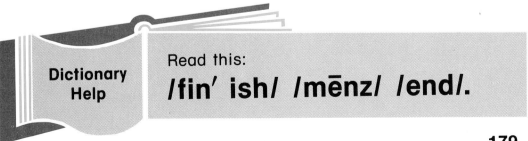

Dictionary Help

Read this:

/fin′ ish/ /mēnz/ /end/.

Spelling Helps Reading

Sound out these words. Choose the right words in rows 1 to 7.

vanish	cabin	figure	pedal	planet	record
spirit	damage	lemon	rapid	model	lizard
robin	driven	level	proper	manage	modern

1. **Tree** is to **forest** as **robin** is to....

         a. shower   **b.** birds   **c.** nest

2. **Second** is to **minute** as **inch** is to....

         a. foot   **b.** width   **c.** size

3. **Tin** is to **metal** as **dollar** is to....

         a. figure   **b.** penny   **c.** money

4. **Orange** is to **tree** as **berry** is to....

         a. pie   **b.** petal   **c.** bush

5. **Travel** is to **wagon** as **fly** is to....

         a. pedal   **b.** cabin   **c.** kite

6. **Timid** is to **bold** as **rapid** is to....

         a. slow   **b.** foolish   **c.** limit

7. **Level** is to **even** as **clever** is to....

         a. modest   **b.** stupid   **c.** smart

Chop the long words when you spell;
Then write each little syl-la-ble.

Test

36 *Pumpkin Surprise*

sur prise
com plete
hand ful
sand wich
chil dren
ex claim
help less
thank ful
hun dred
ex plain
king dom
thir sty
ad dress
pump kin
ex tra

Pumpkin *words have the* \VCC CV/ *pattern.*

pump kin/   *We divide* **pumpkin**

VCC CV   *words after the*

12|3   *second consonant.*

Surprise *words have the* \VC CCV/ *pattern.*

sur prise/   *We divide* **surprise**

VC CCV   *words after the*

1|23   *first consonant.*

 1. Write the words that start with /h/.

2. Write the words that are divided after the first consonant letter in the ⟨VC⟩CCV⟩ letter pattern.

3. Write the words that are divided after the second consonant letter in the ⟨VCC⟩CV⟩ letter pattern.

Working with the Words

1. Write the "more than one" picture words.

a.

b.

c.

d.

182

2. Write the words with these starting sounds.

    a. /s/   **b.** /s/

    c. /ch/   **d.** /k/

    e. /k/   **f.** /th/

    g. /th/   **h.** /a/

3. Write the words that <u>end</u> with /s/.

The **a** in **extra** spells a new vowel sound.

We show the vowel sound like this: /ə/.

We call /ə/ a **schwa.**

surprise
complete
handful
sandwich
children
exclaim
helpless
thankful
hundred
explain
kingdom
thirsty
address
pumpkin
extra

4. Write the words that start with **ex.**
Circle the word that ends with the /ə/ sound.

Building Spelling Power

1. helpful or helpless?

2. pump or pumpkin?

3. child or children?

4. dress or address?

5. thirsty or thirty?

6. explain or exclaim?

7. handful or handsome?

8. hungry or hundred?

Dictionary Help

/spel′ ing/ /helps/ /rēd′ ing/.
/rēd′ ing/ /helps/ /spel′ ing/.

184

Spelling Helps Reading

Sound out these VCCCV words.

armful	complain	orchard	simply	partner
ostrich	control	handsome	instant	athlete
monster	entrance	hamster	laundry	farther
improve	darkness	antlers	concrete	explore

Write each scrambled sentence correctly on paper.
Mark each sentence **True** or **False.** Tell why.

1. make pets hamsters good.
2. concrete made all sidewalks are of.
3. very birds are handsome ostriches.
4. hardware pickles are stores sold in.
5. improve athletes try their skills to good.
6. grown orchards in oranges and apples are.
7. in laundries to work not people allowed are.
8. seldom they sell merchants complaints get goods about.
9. pumpkin turkey pie and thankful remind the Pilgrims of us.
10. stands at hundreds dog hot sandwiches of children purchase.

That's all
Till next fall.

Test

SPELLING CONSONANT SOUNDS

/b/

ball

/d/

dog

/f/

fish

/g/

girl

/h/

hat

/l/

lamp

/m/

moon

/n/

nail

/p/

pig

/r/

rabbit

/t/

turtle

/v/

vase

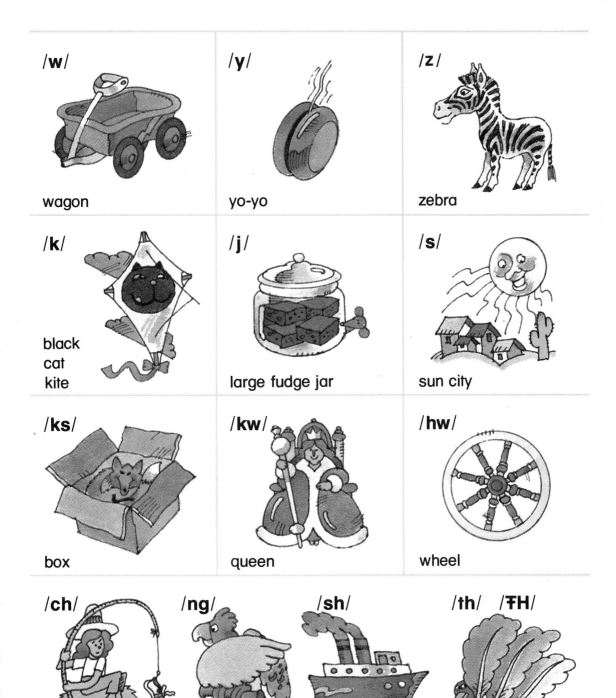

/w/ wagon

/y/ yo-yo

/z/ zebra

/k/ black cat kite

/j/ large fudge jar

/s/ sun city

/ks/ box

/kw/ queen

/hw/ wheel

/ch/ such-a-catch

/ng/ pink wing

/sh/ ship

/th/ /ŦH/ three feathers

187

SPELLING VOWEL SOUNDS

/a/

Fat Cat

/e/

Red Hen

/i/

Big Pig

/o/   /ô/

Hot Dog

/u/

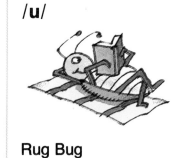

Rug Bug

/ā/

Play
Train Game

/ē/

See Me Eat

/ī/

Find
My
Fine
Bright Tie

/ō/

No Old Show
Boat Smoke

/ū/   /ü/

Cute New
Blue Suits

/ou/

Loud Crowd

/oi/

Toy Noise

/ô/

Maud's
Small Shawl

/u̇/

Good Book

/ü/

Cool Goose

/är/

Barn Yard

/ãr/

Hair Care

/ėr/

Her Girl Curl

/ir/

Hear Cheer

/ôr/

More
Short Boards

/ə/

About
Taken
Lemon
Pencil
Circus

SOFT ENDINGS

/əl/

Final
Nickel
Pickle

/ər/

Better
Color
Collar

/ē/

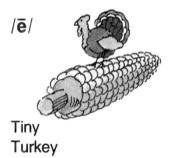

Tiny
Turkey

189

ᔥTHE SNURKSᔥ

The following list contains the snurks that appear in the 36 units of this book. The numeral following each word shows the unit in which the snurk appears.

above 33	comb 24	half 24	paste 13	though 17
again 33	couldn't 21	heard 23	people 28	thought 17
ahead 33	countries 26	heart 20	pour 17	through 17, 23
almost 32	country 26	heavy 25	prove 10	today 29
among 33	course 17	instead 29	proving 10	tomorrow 30
another 27	dead 7	into 29	quiet 5	touch 17
answer 27	don't 21	lead 22	rein 23	tough 17
anyone 30	early 25	learn 18	rough 17	trouble 28
anything 30	earn 18	lose 10	search 18	truth 14
bear 23	earth 18	losing 10	sew 22	waste 13
become 34	eight 23	love 10	shove 10	wear 20
bought 17	every 25	loving 10	shoving 10	weigh 22
bread 7	everyone 30	mirror 27	sign 24	weight 23
break 23	everything 30	money 35	someone 30	whole 23
breakfast 30	fought 17	monkey 32	something 30	wild 8
brother 27	four 22	most 9	sometime 30	won't 21
brought 17	fourth 17, 23	neighbor 27	son 22	world 19
busy 25	front 1	none 9	soup 17	worries 26
calf 24	grandfather 30	nothing 29	sugar 27	worry 26
cherries 26	grandmother 30	once 12	sure 4	worse 19
cherry 26	great 6	only 25	taste 13	your 22
child 8	group 17	ought 17	tear 20	you're 21, 22
				yourself 30